STORY MAMA

What Children's Stories Teach Us
About Life, Love, and Mothering

AMY RUTH HENRY

For my mamas-in-training:
Emily, Anna, and Elenia

Copyright © 2013 Amy Ruth Henry.

All rights reserved. Published by Brambleberry Press.

This book was formerly published under the title *Humpty Dumpty Just Needed a Nap*.

No part of this publication may be reproduced, or stored in a retrieval system, or transmitted in any form or by any means, electronic, mechanical, photocopying, recording, or otherwise, without written permission of the publisher. For information regarding permission, email admin@wholemama.com.

ISBN-13: 978-0-615-88126-3

10 9 8 7 6 5 4 3 2   11 12 13 14 15

Printed in the U.S.A.
Second softcover edition, September 2013

Cover & interior design: J.S. White

Table of Contents

In Which We Make Introductions	1
Winnie-the-Pooh—Which Hundred Acre Mama are You?	5
The Little Engine That Could—Pace Yourself	10
The Three Bears—Parent In That "Just Right" Place	15
The Pied Piper of Hamelin—Follow the Beat of Your Own, uh, Piper	18
Cinderella—Stop Waiting For Prince Charming	22
Owl Babies—The Power of Mama Love	26
Owl Babies Bonus—Baby O'Mine	30
Monday's Child—Children Are As Different As the Days of the Week	33
Make Way For Ducklings—Train Your Ducklings	36
Make Way for Ducklings Bonus—Teach Them to Fish	40
The Story of Ferdinand—Accept Your Children For Who They Are	42
Stone Soup—Many Hands Make Light Work	46
Green Eggs and Ham—Respect Your Child's Personhood	51
Mike Mulligan and His Steam Shovel—Be a Good Finder	55
The Mitten—Know Your Limits	58
The Mitten Bonus—Ten Commandments for Mama-Care	63
Olivia—Imagination Stirs When Boredom Occurs	64
The Giving Tree—Don't Be a Martyr	69

The Velveteen Rabbit—Be Real	74
The Saggy Baggy Elephant—Make Peace With Your Body	78
We're Going On a Bear Hunt—Sometimes You Just Gotta Go Through It	82
Julius: The Baby of the World—Don't Play Favorites	86
Tootle—Channel Their Energy	90
Curious George—Keep the Leash Short	93
Curious George Bonus—Don't Die on Molehills	97
Mary, Mary Quite Contrary—Paint or Get Off the Ladder	99
Where the Wild Things Are—Monsters: They're Not Just For Children Anymore	102
Harold and the Purple Crayon—Bend or Break	107
Alexander and the Terrible, Horrible, No Good, Very Bad Day—The Gift of a Bad Day	111
The Taming of the Shrew—A Short Treatise on PMS	115
Frog and Toad are Friends—We All Need Ya-Yas	118
The Magic Fish—Be Content	122
The Magic Fish Bonus—Those Darned Joneses	127
If You Give a Mouse a Cookie—Nip Whining in the Bud	130
Horton Hatches the Egg—Say What You Mean and Mean What You Say	134
Good Dog, Carl—Talk Less	138
The Emperor's New Clothes—Have the Courage to Hear the Truth	141
The Emperor's New Clothes Bonus—Hester and His Perpetually Doting Mother	145

Miss Nelson is Missing—What To Do When Your Ship Mutinies	148
Miss Nelson is Missing Bonus—Battle Now or War Later	151
The Ugly Duckling—There Is No Such Thing as a Misfit	154
The Runaway Bunny—Call Their Bluff	157
The Runaway Bunny Bonus—I. Do. Not. Negotiate. With. Terrorists.	160
The Gingham Dog and the Calico Cat—Avoid Silly Arguments	162
Millions of Cats—Choose Your Commitments Wisely	165
Humpty Dumpty—How To Prevent Great Falls	169
Humpty Dumpty Bonus—The Secret of Mothering, Revealed	173
Chicken Little—What if the Sky *Isn't* Falling?	176
The Very Hungry Caterpillar—Don't Be Afraid of Change	179
The Country Bunny—Work Yourself Out of a Job	183
The Little House—The Seasons of Motherhood	188
The Three Little Pigs—Prepare for the Empty Pigpen	194
There Was an Old Woman Who Lived in a Shoe—Enjoy Those Babies	197
Miss Rumphius—Make the World a Better Place	200
Miss Rumphius Bonus—Plan Your 75th Birthday Party	205
Madeline—Embrace Your Scars	208
Your Story—Epilogue	212

> "As you grow ready for it,
> somewhere or other you will find
> what is needful for you in a book."

GEORGE MACDONALD, SCOTTISH AUTHOR (1824-1905)

nce upon a time, in a land not so far away, there lived a mother who had no idea what she was doing.

Despite having helped raise her four younger siblings and having managed a thriving babysitting business in the late 80s, she had no clue what to do when it came to parenting her own children. What, for example, was the appropriate response when a child refused to leave the store without a gum ball in his mouth? Or when each and every one of her children refused to eat their broccoli? She had heard of Mountains and Molehills, but how, pray tell, was a body to tell the difference between the two?

If only she had a fairy godmother who would sweep down, wave her magic wand, and give her a ball gown of patience, a glass slipper of wisdom, a stagecoach full of ideas for keeping her children occupied on the twenty-fifth rainy day in a row. Oh, how prepared for the mothering ball she would be.

But, alas, despite her desperate pleas, no fairy godmother appeared. Her own mother had parented too long ago to remember essentials like What Happens When We Don't Burp the Baby and Why We No Longer Put Brandy On A Baby's Gums. Her grandmother was even less helpful, recalling only that children liked butterscotch candies, one after the other in quick succession. To add insult to maternal injury, the parenting books the woman read were often written by people as far removed from mothering as a person could be: Men.

Who then would help this woman traverse the moat of ignorance and enter the castle of confidence? Who, or what, would rescue her from the stone turret of doubt, the dungeon of despair? Who would protect her from the spinning needle of poor decision-making?

As often happens in such tales, her answer came from a most unexpected source. It wasn't a prince on a noble steed or a magic spell or the twinkling of somebody's nose: It was the shelf full of children's books right smack in the middle of her living room. Was it possible that these classic stories, fairy tales, folk tales, and Mother Goose rhymes were the key to the door mysteriously marked "Mothering Secrets for the Information Deprived?" Perhaps she did have a fairy godmother looking out for her after all....

Without hesitation, the mother delved into the books and found that, sprinkled with a wee bit of pixie dust, these tales (sneakily disguised as "toddler entertainers" and "long-winter-afternoon fillers") indeed held a mother lode of parenting gold.

Between countless loads of dirty laundry and a strenuous peanut butter sandwich-making schedule, all record of her quest might have been lost had she not done one very important thing: She took notes.

In Which We Make Introductions

"How do you spell 'love?'" —Piglet
"You don't spell it…you feel it." —Pooh
A.A. MILNE

s you have probably guessed, that mother is me. And, because I don't want to wear my dear reader out with endless repetitions of "my seventeen-year-old son" or "my nine-year-old daughter," here is a tiny twist on a familiar story to help introduce the people who so kindly allowed me to use them as writing fodder:

If you can, for a moment, imagine a Hundred Acre Wood slightly different from the one you usually have in mind when you think of Pooh, Piglet, Rabbit, Owl, Tigger, Eeyore, Kanga, and Roo.

In this alternate story, my husband, Ian, plays the role of

Christopher Robin, the coolest head romping about the Wood in his galoshes. If ever a problem arises amongst the varied and mostly ridiculous inhabitants, Christopher Robin is who we call upon to calmly dispense a dose of sense and a bit of ballast to the situation. And not only sense, but practical help, such as How To Turn Off The Smoke Alarm and Reaching The Dishes On The Top Shelf. Just like in the original Pooh stories, Christopher Robin's arrival home at the end of the work day is always a Most Exciting Event met with Great Rejoicing.

Although I wish I could be compared to the lovely and gracious Kanga, I'm afraid my Hundred Acre *döppelganger* is Owl. Like him, I wear glasses and am bossy and opinionated. I flutter about the Wood pontificating about subjects no one else cares about ("Owl hasn't exactly got Brain, but he Knows Things.") and can be regularly found giving advice no one heeds. However, Christopher Robin insists he loves Owl and sometimes you just have to take things like that at Face Value.

Granted, it's an odd match, but one that has worked, more or less, for the better part of a quarter century. The interspecies bond has produced a half dozen progeny, each, like their parents, resembling a Hundred Acre character.

Emily (18) is our Tigger. Cheerful and bubbly, she loves fun, people, singing, and—being born just before Halloween—owls. In fact, for several years I tried to turn her into an Owl like me, but she would have none of it. Owls don't bounce, you see, and Em is, above all, bouncy. It took me awhile to figure this out, but now I am most grateful for my sweet Tigger girl who writes songs, adores children, and wears frightfully unique outfits.

Her brother, Austen (17), is our resident Winnie-The-

Pooh. He isn't wildly excited about being compared to a stuffed bear, but it can't be helped: In writing, one must be, above all, honest. Loving, sweet, cuddly, and never without a dramatic story to tell, Austen's worst gripe in life so far is that he was named after a nineteenth-century female romance writer. So I promised him I would also tell you that he leads his Boy Scout Troop and rows crew like a boss. We no longer wrestle because I like living.

Since, as Pooh so aptly put it, "It's so much better with two," we have Benjamin (15) as our Piglet. Just like in the books, our Piglet and Pooh are rarely seen apart. Though life is sometimes scary, Piglet and Pooh stick together, even when the water is rising and Christopher Robin and Owl aren't on deck to solve their problems. A hot wing lover given to infectious fits of laughter, Ben is our forest's tech guy, the one we call to find out What Happened to Firefox And Where Did The File To My New Book Disappear To.

Anna-Sophia (13) stars in our tale as Rabbit. She likes cleanliness, properly set tables, and a finely-honed schedule. Resident linen-closet organizer, baker, splinter remover, and vocalist, Anna's goal in life is to find out if there is any need in the world for an opera-singing emergency room doctor.

Our personal A.A. Milne, Elenia (9), is the author of the bunch. Quiet and reserved (except for late-night silliness on the weekends), the bespeckled Elenia has read her way through most of our extensive library and can be called on to expound upon things like Which Bennett Sister Is The Prettiest and Why Heathcliff Didn't Just Marry Cathy When He Had the Chance. When not reading, she's pounding out stories on her

1931 portable Royal typewriter.

Cooper (7) is our Roo. Energetic, bossy, and louder than an ungreased freight train, he wasn't quite what we expected in our old age. He loves *Star Wars* and Legos and trying my patience. He also loves "boy nights" with his brothers that consist of candy, movies, candy, wrestling until someone cries and/or bleeds, and candy.

Depending on the day or the phase of the moon, each of us takes turns being Eeyore, for what would a family be without the lovable depressive? Besides, no one wanted to be pigeoned into *that* particular hole.

Now that you know everyone a bit, in the words of A.A. Milne himself, "…perhaps the best thing to do is to stop writing Introductions and get on with the book."

The Pooh Story Book

BY A.A. MILNE

"The things that make me different are the things that make me."

ike I mentioned, I liken myself to Owl and most of the time that's true. Owl Mamas like me fall so easily into pontification that sometimes our friends run or suddenly act busy when they see us coming. Owl is such a know-it-all you can hardly blame them.

But, although I possess a good bit of Owl, it's also true that I have some serious Rabbit moments, freaking out over things like throwing up and germs and not getting enough greens into my bunnies. My Rabbit self keeps Germ-X in all our cars and insists hands are washed whenever we've been out and that no one uses a green cutting board for dicing raw chicken or a red cutting board to chop cilantro.

Owl+Rabbit doesn't really sum up my mothering completely, though. For that, you'd have to add in a good dose of Eeyore. Raised by a father whose idea of a fun time was a day spent pulling up weeds by the root, can you blame me for often feeling that my cup is one half—no, wait—one quarter full? Life is tough, says my Eeyore self, might as well accept it. Ho hum.

But, Owl+Rabbit+Eeyore doesn't define me either, because I'm also in good part Piglet, worrying my way through life and hoping that Pooh will show up at opportune times like when I'm getting munchy or when I'm in need of a cheering song. Piglet's fragile nerves are what I blame for only recently allowing Austen to drive me the mile to Walmart, even though he has had his driver's license for more than eighteen months.

Then again, Owl+Rabbit+Eeyore+Piglet doesn't do me justice either. Sometimes, say, when the moon is full or the stars are aligned just so, I manage to be as calm and cool as Christopher Robin, with a ready answer for any problem that takes place in my personal Hundred Acre. It is my Christopher Robin alter-ego that suggests Turning Off The Water When The Toilet Is Overflowing and Making Sure The Flue Is Open Before Lighting Fires.

But the Owl+Rabbit+Eeyore+Piglet+Christopher Robin mix falls short, because Pooh plays into the mix, too. Despite his rare appearance, the relaxed me, the brain-full-of-fluff me is in there...somewhere. At times even Owls can be relaxed. Even Owls can be friendly. Even Owls can occasionally offer a Smackeral of Something to someone who's rumbly in their tumbly without worrying if it's eco-friendly or locally grown.

On good days, I can even be a Tigger Mama, suggesting something fun like climbing the highest tree in the Wood or bouncing somebody into a river. No mama wants to be an ogre, not even mamas who are primarily Owls and Rabbits.

It's still not as good as Kanga, though.

About as often as a sighting of Mars or, say, Haley's Comet, I can even pull off a little of her action. Quintessential mama that marsupial is...gentle, calming, kindness always on her tongue. How many times I would gladly banish all the other members of the Wood from my personality if only the Author Himself would give me more Kanga.

But alas, it is not to be (sigh). More days than not, sweet Kanga eludes me: Owl is too busy giving advice. Rabbit is too busy nagging. Eeyore is too busy sighing, and Piglet is too busy fretting to let sweet Kanga have much say in this mothering business. Even Christopher Robin can get in her way, offering answers instead of empathy, fixing things when all my little ones want is Kanga's loving ear and some warm cookies.

Do you ever beat yourself up for being more Rabbit Mama than Kanga Mama? More Eeyore than Tigger? More Piglet than Pooh?

Me, too. In fact, I consider it a good day when I'm 60% Rabbit and only 40% Eeyore. It's a better day when I'm 75% Owl and 25% Pooh. And even better when I'm 5% Kanga, 15% Christopher Robin, only 30% Rabbit and an odd smattering of the others. If the percentage of Eeyore isn't too high on that particular day, I am even happy with that meager 5% Kanga. Way too deep into this mothering business to back out, I'm learning that even Eeyore, with his deep brooding thoughts and mercurial moods, has his place.

Point is, just like every member living in the burrows, the tree holes, the branches, or the sticks of the Hundred Acre Wood, mamas are different from each other. You may be a vegan mama who shops at Whole Foods. You may be a skirt sporting, tennis shoe wearing mama from Iowa who cans all her own peaches. You may be a Greenwich Village mama who doesn't own a car, much less a car seat, for your little one.

But, from the burrows to the burbs, from forests to metropolises, from hand washing our kids' underwear against a rock in a river to throwing it in a Whirlpool front-loading washing machine with Downy Mountain Fresh fabric softener, all Hundred Acre mamas have this one thing in common: We love our kids.

We love our kids.

And it's a good thing. For, without mama love, who could possibly do the things we're expected to do? Slather cream over a sore bottom, clean up vomit, read aloud for an *entire hour?*

So, you're Pooh. She's Rabbit. I'm Owl. That calm chic over there? She's the enviable Kanga. So what? Depending on the day, time of month, season of life, we're also everything in between, smash-ups in the Wood, all of us doing the very best we can.

In the end, all Hundred Acre mamas are doing the same thing, being *exactly* who we were made to be, *exactly* who our children need us to be. At times strict like Rabbit. At others, wise like Owl. At still others, a party animal like Tigger.

So, let's all stop blubbering that we're not patient like Kanga and quit berating ourselves for not being easygoing like Pooh or organized like Rabbit and get busy being whatever kind of mamas we were meant to be.

Even if that Mama is, on her best days, 75% Eeyore.

The Little Engine That Could

By Watty Piper

"I think I can—I think I can—I think I can..."

"uff, puff, puff. Toot, toot, toot. Ding dong, ding dong." So begins Watty Piper's beloved tale. A train full of toys and dolls breaks down, leaving them all wondering how they are going to get over the mountain to deliver their goods to the little girls and boys on the other side. Several times they are almost rescued by other engines, but, each time, the trains have some excuse for why they can't help. One is too old and tired. One is too overqualified to be of assistance. One is much too important for such lowly work.

Then comes along the Little Blue Engine. Her only job so far has been changing trains in the train yard, so she's not sure she's strong enough to help, but, at the begging of the animals and dolls, she decides to try. They hitch up the train and up the mountain she goes, pulling the load, straining her engine, not sure if she has what it takes to get the train over the mountain. But, with a lot of hard work and perseverance, and to the delight of the toys, she does just that, eventually cresting the summit saying, "I thought I could, I thought I could, I thought I could."

* * *

Mamas are a lot like the Little Blue Engine. We, too, when starting out, have no idea how or even *if* we can pull this mothering thing off. We're newbies in the train yard, our motors untested, our wheels untried. Just like no train knows innately how to pull up a steep mountain pass without overheating or how to chug downhill without burning out its brakes, no woman comes into the world knowing exactly how to be a mom. There are no classes for things like "How To Know When To Call the Doctor" or "Is this mole/rash/attitude/smell normal?" A lot of the time, we're just winging it.

But, just as the Little Blue Engine didn't allow his lack of knowledge, expertise, or experience keep him from giving his best, neither should we. He didn't allow his puny size to interfere with the bigger mission—getting the toys and goodies over the hill. Nor did his enthusiasm lag when he looked at the size of the train and heard the army of small voices begging him for help.

What if mamas could be like this? What if we refused to look ahead to the grade of the hill or the possible mechanical failures that could waylay us or to what we'll need to do if we need repairs halfway through the journey? What if we neither obsessed about our unpreparedness nor fretted about our puny amount of experience? What if we simply focused on what the Little Engine did: Conquering the stinking hill.

The hill being, of course, raising a lovely bunch of coconuts.

But it's a long haul, this mothering thing, and one thing this story teaches us is to think of it more as a marathon than as a sprint. The Little Engine, if anything, *persevered*.

My sister-in-law is a runner who recently read a book that changed the way she ran. Before reading this book, like most runners, she ran every day without fail. However, not only were her race times refusing to budge, but she was constantly in some sort of pain. The book told her to (get this): Run *less*. That's right. Instead of pounding the pavement day after day, the author recommended running only three days a week and incorporating other exercises like weight lifting and swimming on non-running days. The result? Not only are her race times improving, her feet, knees, and hips are feeling better than they have in years.

Some people call motherhood a marathon because they see it as a long row to hoe, a long, protracted exercise in pain. As such, they encourage us to grit our teeth, lower our chins, and forge ahead, ignoring the blisters on our heels or the stitch in our sides.

I like my sister-in-law's approach better. Rather than running at full tilt each and every day, parenting should be run in intervals, with lots of variety and plenty of rest days in between. Doing so can prevent injuries and help us conserve energy for the calf-burning hills and the final sprint toward the finish line. Surely the Little Engine wasn't barreling up that mountain at full steam, but conserving energy, pacing herself carefully on the journey.

Pacing, however, can be as hard to remember as the daily application of sun screen and I, for one, struggle miserably at both.

When I first started hauling my mothering load uphill, I was as arrogant as the Freight Train, as stubborn as the Streamliner, as ignorant as the Little Blue Engine. After Emily's birth, I gave myself exactly one day to recover before driving an hour to the commissary and standing in line for 45 minutes to buy my groceries. Before my milk came in, we had visited both sets of parents, my grandparents, and received approximately ten sets of well-intentioned visitors. Every day I woke while it was still dark and had done a full day of work before nine am. By the time Emily was three months old, I had sewed her several tiny dresses, read every baby book on the market, and planned out the course of her life. I did this, not because I liked it, but because this is what I thought good mothers were supposed to do.

If only I had known to mother like the Little Engine, advancing down the track one 'step' at a time, looking forward only as far as my energy allowed, not borrowing trouble, hoping for the best, knowing that some day I would round the corner and find myself at the top of the mountain.

If I had, I would have known to sandwich slow days between busy ones. I would have known I needed trashy beach reads between 400-page biographies. I would have known to invite a bunch of passengers to cheer me along as I panted,

"I think I can—I think I can—I think I can." I would have realized that no one, not even mamas, can run a marathon at a six-minute-mile pace. Well, if you're one of those super skinny runner types, you can, but sometimes they drop dead inexplicably, so let's stick with the pacing concept.

My point is: The Little Engine taught me not to push myself so hard at the beginning of the trip that I wore out by the time my kids got out of diapers. She helped me figure out where I needed to sprint and where I could slow down to a walk. Even now, she reminds me to tuck an energy bar into my pocket so I have something for the end. And for the middle. And for that one hilly section that always kicks my butt.

Maybe, if I continue to learn from her, one of these days I'll be able to look back over my smokestack and say, *"I thought I could, I thought I could, I thought I could."*

Goldilocks and the Three Bears

FOLK TALE

oldilocks knew what a lot of mamas don't: That being too hard or too soft was no good and that what a body really needed was what Baby Bear had, something "just right."

Mama Softie, for example, adores her children. They are the light of her life, the sparkle in her eye. She lives and breathes solely for her offspring. A kind woman, Mama Softie goes out of her way to fix special foods, to soothe sorrows, to scratch up her own legs in her attempt to pave a smooth path for her babies. Her children's birthday parties are always the best ones. She hand stitches heart doilies for the tea party, frosts petit fours until the wee sma's, and squeezes the lemonade by hand because that's the way they like it.

But, sadly, despite her Herculean efforts, Mama Softie is not appreciated much. Her children take her for granted and throw fits when their special needs are not attended to in a timely fashion. They sometimes wallop Mama Softie in the stomach and have been known to grind a heavy boy heel into her tender foot. If she slacks in her vigilance, all hell breaks loose. Demands rain from the upper bedrooms, tantrums occur when she says the forbidden word (No), and, when she gets sick, no one really cares except when they realize, hey, it's Friday night—where, for the love of all that's holy, is our homemade pizza?

Her sister, Harsh Mama, doesn't make these kinds of mistakes. She runs her home like a Marine Corps installation. When she cracks her whip, you better heave to, because consequences are brutal and doled out with unfaltering precision. Harsh Mama has a harsh voice to match her name. Sadly, her kids are immune to it, so it doesn't have quite the effect it used to. Which, of course, means she must get harsher and harsher just to get people to budge.

On the surface, Harsh Mama is treated with more respect than Softie Mama, but it is a respect born of fear, not love. Her children kowtow to her only until they are big enough to fight back against her particular form of bullying. They often rebel against such tight constraints and, because she has pulled out all the stops for minor infractions such as not eating their eggs or putting too much ranch dressing on their salad, her children are also deaf to her directives concerning major issues like returning the car unscratched and not coming home pregnant at seventeen.

It is more difficult to locate than the magnetic South Pole, but we might as well *try* to parent in that "just right" Baby Bear place. The women I know who seem to be the most cheerful and confidant moms with the happiest, healthiest children, are the ones who balance strictness with a generous dose of love and affection. They demand obedience, but, in between disciplining sessions, laugh with their children, roll on the floor being silly, and crawl into bed with them to listen to their stories. Being strict without being loving is for boot camp, not for home. But being too soft to properly establish rules and boundaries is like feeding children a pure sugar diet: Fun at first, but disappointingly short-lived.

So, the next time you tell your kids the story of The Three Bears, keep an eye on Goldilocks. She may look innocent enough with her blond curly locks and her precocious determination, but she's a smart one. Watch how she eschews extremes on both sides and settles (quite literally) into middle ground.

If you sense you may be mothering on the poles like Mama Softie and Harsh Mama, imagine yourself walking through the Bear home. See the bowls of too hot and too cold and just right porridge on the table. Observe the too hard chair and the too soft chair and the just right chair in the living room. Creep upstairs and find Goldilocks sleeping peacefully, not in the big, hard Papa Bear bed, nor the too soft Mama Bear bed, but in Baby Bear's "just right" one.

Just don't forget to skedaddle before Ursa Major, Ursa Minor, and their kid come home and find you sniffing around their crib.

The Pied Piper of Hamelin

Fairy Tale

The Pied Piper of Hamelin, cheated by the townspeople, got his revenge when he played a tune so sweet that it caused their children to follow him blindly out of the village, down the road, and into a dark cave where they were never seen again.

We can shake our heads at the sad story and console ourselves that *our* children would never do such a thing, and hopefully they won't, but I can tell you that, as a mom, I have followed blindly, like those children did, more times than I care to admit.

When I had Emily, I had no idea what I was doing. Since several of my friends were in love with a certain parenting philosophy (let's call it *The Way*), I bought into it and hungrily devoured the books and tapes that taught its philosophy. Thanks to these tapes I learned that my baby was hell-bent on turning me into her indentured servant and that my job was to resist her at every turn. *The Way* taught me that Emily was a selfish, narcissistic little blood sucker who would take an infantile mile for every maternal inch I gave her. I was advised to take heed.

I followed *The Way* religiously and it was working beautifully until the day two-week-old Emily began to cry in her crib.

"Stop," I told Ian, when he got out of bed to get her. "This is what They said would happen."

"Who?" he said.

"*The Way*," I said.

"What would happen?" he said.

"Manipulation," I said.

"By a *baby?*" he said.

"I nursed her just fifteen minutes ago," I explained. "She's absolutely fine. If we give in to her now, the next thing you know, she'll be texting us for more cash from the mall across the street, claiming she's 'hungry.' Don't do it."

Backed by the wisdom of *The Way*, and to my Great Chagrin, we steeled ourselves against the sound of her crying.

But after an hour, I couldn't take it anymore. I was weak, what can I say? A failure.

Throwing off my covers, I ran to her bedroom across the hall, only to find that her newborn cap had unrolled itself all the way down to her chubby little chin. My sweet baby was thrashing around her bassinet in terror.

Horrified, I swept her up like a woman rescuing her child from drowning and cradled her in my arms the rest of the night, my pathetic attempt at penance for being such a

Terrible, Terrible Mommy.

And here's where the story gets ugly, because I didn't learn my lesson. It took me several more children before I realized that *The Way* didn't have all the answers. Neither did any other formula. Before it was all over, I had bought into Homemade Bread Baking, The Eschewment of Birth Control, Going Without Pain Medication In Childbirth Even Though We Live in One Of the Most Medically Advanced Nations in the World, Sewing All My Children's Clothes, Wooden Toys Only, and The Abandonment of Novel Reading Because It Is Frivolous and Selfish.

And, as Emily grew, instead of riding the wave of her bouncy and impetuous social butterfly-ness, I squashed her. At the tender age of three-and-a-half, she was sitting at the kitchen table, suffering through phonics and penmanship, this girl who could barely hold a pencil in her soft little hand. As I write this, I am refilled with guilt, but have only myself to blame. What can I say? I bought into many different (and sometimes wildly opposing) parenting philosophies because I was afraid of trusting my own gut, because I was determined to do it better than my own mother had, because I felt Mothering Utopia was out there, somewhere, if only I could find it.

There's nothing inherently wrong with seeking the counsel of mothers who have gone before us, I've long since learned. The Proverbs tell us that there is wisdom in a multitude of counselors and it is true, as anyone who has ever lived near their multitude knows. Our mothers and grandmothers and aunts and older friends can be one of our greatest sources of support, encouragement, and guidance as we mother our children. But, as the parents of Hamelin painfully learned, not in lieu of thinking. Even a grandmother's advice can be wrong. Our own mothers parented a long time ago; lots of things have changed since then. Following any one person's advice may lead us to parent like they did, which isn't necessarily like we should. Depending on our Facebook buddies to tell us how to parent may do the same.

So, rather than absorbing every jot and tittle of advice we hear on one extreme, and refusing any counsel whatsoever on the other, perhaps we should embrace parts of both while making space for our own conclusions. Your mother probably doesn't remember the details of how to potty train a resistant toddler. Your grandmother doesn't either. But one or both of them may recall in vivid detail what they wish they'd done differently with their teenagers. Rather than blindly following the Piper, perhaps we'd be better off to listen to counsel, and filter out the good from the not-so-good using the brain God gave us for just such occasions.

Embrace the best. Toss the rest. That's what my brain is telling me. What is yours telling you?

Cinderella

Fairy Tale

Cinderella is such a household name that we may forget how she got it. The stepdaughter of a cruel woman, she was forced to do the family's chores, including, but not limited to, cleaning out the fireplace. One morning, the evil stepmother found her so worn out from her chores that she had fallen asleep in the cold cinders she hadn't yet cleaned up. Thus, the mocking nickname, Cinderella.

Today, the term "Cinderella" refers not just to the fairy tale, but to anyone who rises from the "ashes." The movie Cinderella Man *is about how boxer Jimmy Braddock's came back after a long losing streak to become the world heavyweight champion from 1935 to 1937. Pop artist, Adele, recently had a Cinderella come-back of her own: Diagnosed with a vocal cord hemorrhage in October, 2011, she went on to win five Grammy awards in 2012, including Album of the Year, Record of the Year, and Song of the Year.*

If anyone needed a come-back, it was Cinderella. Sorely abused by her stepmother, she prays to be rescued. That rescuing comes in the form of a fairy godmother who magically makes it possible for Cinderella to attend the royal ball. There, Cinderella attracts the eye of the prince, but before he finds out who she is, the clock starts to strike midnight, the hour the fairy godmother's magic is supposed to wear off. In her haste to get away, Cinderella drops one of her glass slippers. The prince, smitten with the nameless beauty, scours the countryside looking for the one who fits that shoe. Despite the evil stepmother's attempts to keep Cinderella from being discovered, the prince insists that she try the shoe on, even though she is only a char maid. And—oh joy!—it fits. The prince takes Cinderella away from her cruel stepmother to his castle where they marry and live happily ever after.

lthough Cinderella is a lovely example of a "comeback" story, sadly, it has possibly made more women miserable than any other fairy tale on record; the whole "One day my prince will come" philosophy being a subtle way of saying, "As soon as I have the right guy, I can be happy."

Yesterday, Emily and I sat at the pool discussing this. One of her friends has never had a boy interested in her. Another friend just got dumped by her boyfriend of two years. Both girls came to Emily for counsel and she was wondering what to say.

"Ultimately, what do you think they want?" I asked her.

"They want to be happy," she said. "And they think having a boyfriend will make them happy. Instead of improving themselves or preparing for life, they are living only to get a man, as if that will fulfill them and fix all their problems."

My father used to say "There is nothing more attractive to a man than a woman who doesn't need him." What he meant was that a whole, secure, and interesting woman is, in princess speak, *enchanting*. But a lot of women look to marriage to do what Emily's friends hoped it would, to make them whole, fill the void, and bring about their perfect happiness. Half the movies in the world tell that disappointing story. Sure, for the few first years of romantic bliss, it may seem that finding our prince has solved our troubles, but what happens when the days of having no other responsibilities other than staring into each other's eyes are over?

In my humble opinion, many times when moms complain about motherhood and the mundane tasks associated with it, what they are really complaining about is the lack of intellectual stimulation, creative outlet, and relational connectivity they had in their pre-baby days. They whine that hubby is late from work and wants to play with his buddies on the weekend not because they want to control him or don't want him to have fun, but because they think that it's his job to wander the countryside in hot pursuit of his princess, to woo her into his handsome arms, and to take her away where he will make all her dreams come true.

But it's not. No man, no matter how princely, can do that. With the help of the Almighty, it's *our* job to make our dreams come true. And that's where the problem lies: Give a new mom an afternoon off to do whatever she wants to do and watch her do…*nothing*. Without diapers to change and play dates to arrange and sippy cups to rinse, mom doesn't know what to do with herself. Interrupted an average of five times a minute for years on end, her focusing muscles have atrophied along with her formerly toned gluteus maximus.

Some moms have been moms for so long they no longer recognize themselves. What had been a sassy, bandana and hoop-earring-wearing gypsy is now a befuddled, yoga pant and ratty t-shirt sporting bore, as interested and as interesting as a newly filled Pamper. If we're not careful, we can lose sight of our passions and our senses of humor. Then we wonder why motherhood doesn't deliver.

What we need, perhaps, is a Cinderella comeback of our own, a way to boost our enchantment factor so that we aren't putting life on hold because our slipper-toting prince hasn't shown up yet or *has* shown up, but in a ten-year-old minivan.

Walt Disney would shiver in his grave at the suggestion, but what if we stopped waiting around for a man (or a baby) to fulfill us and got busy living? What if we dove into pottery, stained-glass, yoga, website design, Thai cooking, screen printing, calligraphy, poetry, clothing design, knitting, watercolor painting, salsa dancing, growing strawberries, making our own baby food, composting, cutting hair, breeding Golden Retrievers, golfing, running, swimming, biking, writing children's stories, black and white photography, growing organic produce, baking homemade croissants, typesetting, jewelry making, antique collecting, letter writing, glass blowing, and, my personal favorite…reading? My guess is, if we delved into a few of these, even without castles and jewels and golden crowns, we would be rich. Husbands and babies would be the cherry on an already delicious frosted cupcake.

Marriage is, or can be, a great, fulfilling venture. Same with mothering. But having a prince does not a magical life necessarily make. No person should bear the burden of having to bring about another person's penultimate happiness. If we truly want to live "happily ever after," *we*—not the prince—need to be the charming one.

Owl Babies

By Martin Waddell

"I want my mommy!" said Bill.

Owlets Sarah, Percy, and Bill wake up one day in their tree and realize their mother is gone. Where is she? When will she be back? What if she doesn't come back? They ponder different answers to those questions and worry all night long, until, finally, she swoops in from mouse hunting. They are so extraordinarily happy to see her that she asks, "What's all the fuss? You knew I'd come back."

They agree, but we, the readers, know that they hadn't been too certain of that at all.

artin Waddell sounds like a man's name, but he gets mama love so right in his book, *Owl Babies*, it makes you wonder.

Mama love is the strongest love in the world. Watch how a mama flies to her child's bedside at the first sound of a cough. Watch her tuck her children's mittens up into the sleeves of their coats to keep out drafts. See how she plans vegetables into every meal. It's a love summed brilliantly by Tenneva Jordan:

"A mother is a person who seeing there are only four pieces of pie for five people, promptly announces she never did care for pie."

Mamas care about the little things like clean ears and flossed teeth and how many times a week pop is drunk and who has eaten their salad. We want to know not just that our child's day was "okay," but who got to clap the erasers and if Monica was still out sick with step throat. We want the blue book essay answers, not monosyllabic multiple-choice grunts when we ask how they're feeling about that girl or that upcoming football game. We care that the backs of teeth are brushed and that our teens are looking over their shoulders before pulling into oncoming traffic because that's what mama love dictates.

When a child is sad, only mama will do. Sickness is a time when children are especially fragile and in need of mama's tender care. There are so many ways we can provide comfort for our sick ones. We can freshen their beds, make them cozy on the couch, and offer distracting activities. We can see their medications are taken on time, that they have a heating pad, and read them stories. Sickness brings a special vulnerability and children will remember how they were (or were not) cared for during these times.

Sometimes mamas comfort just by their presence alone. Both Ian and I were fortunate to have moms who, short of a natural disaster, were available. If I was at school and not feeling well, knowing mom could jump in the car and come get me often gave me the strength to hold out. After school, I always rushed home with stories of what had happened that day. I couldn't wait to tell her everything, but not everyone has that. One friend told me that she remembers wanting to tell her mother about her day, about her struggles, about the things she was battling, but her mother was always too busy, moving and talking so fast she never sat down with a cup of tea and *listened*.

Even when we are not engaged in riveting, life-changing conversation, our kids need our presence. There is comfort in hearing mom working up in her bedroom, or singing quietly on the porch. Quality time is a myth. Those who have quantity time have (at least the opportunity for) quality time unless they are completely zoned out in front of their screens, say, writing a mothering book.

If you aren't naturally empathetic, motherhood is the time to learn. A child needs his mother's empathy more than almost anything. If he knows her to be an empathetic soul, he will trust and confide in her his whole life. When children fail or falter or ignore our advice, the temptation is to beat them over the head with it. But nothing shuts down a child's spirit faster than a sarcastic, "Well, I knew that would happen. Serves you right." Is your confessional a safe place, a gentle haven of learning, a place of comfort and forgiveness? If so, your children will visit often.

Mama love knows her children's frames. It empties the dishwasher for a teenager who is swamped with homework. It walks the dogs when the dog-walker is feeling under the weather. It relaxes the standards of cleanliness when the family has a rough week because of deadlines, ballet recitals, or play practice. Rules and consistency are great, but without grace, they can be tyrannical. Mama love models tender mercies. It gives children room to cry "uncle" and know we will lend a hand with their project or give them a mental day off from school.

Mama love is what makes our milk come down when we hear someone else's baby cry. It is what gets caught in our throats when we see a child's tiny shoes long after our childbearing years are over. It is what gives cushion to a child's heart so that they can weather life's storms. Mama love is the bedrock of a child's security, the soft landing place for his heart, the fertile soil in which his soul is planted.

It is what gives us the impetus and the drive and the energy to press on year after year. It is not easy work and it is not always rewarding work, but it is *good work*.

Mama love is what makes three owlets cry on a branch for the one who makes life okay, who soothes their most ruffled of feathers, who brings them the yummiest dinners.

Without mama love, we're just babysitting.

Baby O' Mine

he first time you saw her face you could hardly breathe. After all these months of planning and waiting and getting fat with her, suddenly, with hardly any warning, there she was. Your tiny girl. A warm wet jello baby pressed against your worn-out mama heart.

You wondered how she would look, that combination of you and him, and you couldn't even begin to imagine it. But there she was, a beautiful girl, with a perfect wrinkled body, every inch of her so amazing you could do nothing but stare until you feared your eyeballs would dry up. How can this be? How could she—she!—have come out of you? None of your imaginations were even close. Her buttery skin, her raw scratchy fingernails, the fragrance of the top of her head, your almond eyes, his thick head of hair. Later, for months to come, you will be doing dishes or folding Onesies and suddenly it will hit you, that's *your* baby. Half you and half him. Wrapped together in her own pink skin.

You don't know it now, mama, but that girl isn't just a

blank slate, a blob of flesh, a notepad awaiting your maternal scribbling. She's entirely herself, from the thick baby fuzz covering her head to the end of her chubby toes. Not you, not him, but both, and neither, all at once. You'd better buckle your seat belt.

For, as this baby grows, you love her like you never thought you could love anything. You seek to root out any flaw in yourself, so it won't haunt or curse her. You set up feeding and napping schedules and fill pages with every sweet/cute/funny thing she does/says/is. You take videos (twelve in her first three months) and develop boxes of pictures and do everything else you can to capture this, your flesh and blood, your past, your future.

When she is seven days old you fall inexplicably into tears, undone by a pair of tiny ruffled white tights. How soon she will outgrow them! Long before you are ready, she'll be wearing polka dotted ones, thick school girl ones, fishnet ones. And you cry, because no matter what you do, this moment won't last. Those tiny tights will fit only for two weeks. You'll blink and she'll be singing "Tomorrow" at the top of her lungs and going to sleepovers and learning to drive and getting married.

But, despite your best attempts to capture time, it doesn't work. You wake up one day, after years and years of being more tired than a third year medical student and your baby is seventeen. She borrows your makeup and your shaver. You share leggings and jackets. She tells you to wear more brown than black. You tell her to pick her underwear off your bathroom floor. You have girls' nights and secrets you don't tell the brothers or dad. She steals your boots and you pilfer her tank tops. You write up graduation announcements, have a party, watch her sign up for college, fall in love.

So, perhaps a bit grudgingly, you realize that, really, you have just been along for the ride called "Emily." All your control freakishness and your fear and your perfectionism hasn't stopped time and hasn't kept her from growing up.

This girl is your initiation, your guinea pig, your masterpiece, your humbling. She has ushered you into the halls of motherhood with the grace of a butler and the terror of a night time intruder. Never again will you make a decision or think a thought that doesn't figure her into the equation. Never again will you wonder what your purpose on earth is. Never again will you truly sleep…the unknown, the uncontrollable, the utterly perplexing, and the deliciously unpredictable will make sure of that. There's no doubt, your life will never be the same.

Aren't you glad?

Monday's Child

MOTHER GOOSE

Monday's child is fair of face
Tuesday's child is full of grace
Wednesday's child is full of woe
Thursday's child has far to go
Friday's child is loving and giving
Saturday's child works hard for his living
And the child that is born on the Sabbath day
Is bonny and blithe, and good and gay.

ou knew it before they were born, didn't you? Which child would be feisty, which one contemplative; which one would be the sleepyhead, which one the night owl? Before their teeth finished coming in, you had hints as to who would eventually love to build, who would be the story teller, who would be bookish and shy, and who the hub of every party. No matter that they share half their DNA, each child in a family is 100% his or her own self, as different as the days on which they were born.

When I was a young husband hunter, I wrote down a list describing the perfect man. He would be rugged, but tender; sensitive, but strong. He would be a hard worker and like my cooking. He would like dogs and adore children.

Out of all these traits, there are only a few my eventual husband didn't have. (I won't tell you which, but it says "woof.")

We can't pick our children like that, though. Can't write a list, submit it to the Divine, and expect our child delivered to spec. *Oh yes, God. I'll take the extra sweet one with the long, curly, black eyelashes. And, on the side, I'll take a quiet cryer, a long napper, one gifted with self-occupation. For dessert, please make her funny, intelligent, and with a penchant for antiquing.*

Kids don't come as ordered. They arrive in our lives presupposed to liking mustard or hating mayonnaise. This one prefers juice and this one milk. This one likes tuna salad and the other one peanut butter and jelly. This one thinks before speaking. Her sister talks first, then thinks.

The other day I met a woman who had four sisters. She went on and on about what a wonderful, loving mother they had. Wildly curious, my pen poised to take notes, I finally had to ask: "What was it that made her so wonderful?" After giving it some thought she said, "You know, my mother always treated each of us like we were her only child." She knew their likes and dislikes and respected them. When the girls were sick she knew how each one needed to be comforted. She would drop anything if one of them needed a costume sewn or cookies made for school.

That woman knew the power of Monday's Child.

Have a child who hates to read? Monday's Child says don't buy him books for his birthday, even—and especially—if you are an avid reader yourself. Give him Legos. Or a wood burning kit. Or cake decorating supplies. Save the books for the one who reads through them faster than you can check them out at the library. Honor another one for her God-given propensity for organization and give her the job of straightening the linen closet or reorganizing the pantry. Give feet to your son's woodworking dreams by letting him have free reign in the garage to build to his hand's delight. Facilitate another's passion for photography by buying him a camera for Christmas instead of a BB gun. Keep your eyes open for items that perfectly mesh with a child's soap making hobby or passion for beading.

If a child feels understood and loved for exactly who he is, we will have heftier influence when the time comes to smooth off the sharp corners of his personality. A child who does not feel appreciated for his base self will see any attempt to shape him as manipulative. He may go off the deep end to prove a point…he's original! Can't you see??

Hello, Goth.

I have one Monday, two Wednesdays, two Thursdays, and one Friday child. There are two storytellers, one introvert, one who is daring at home and shy in public, and two who could party all day every day and never, ever wear out. Even though there are times I wish I could send one of them back to the factory for new (and improved) parts, would I really want them any other way?

Absolutely not…most days.

Make Way for Ducklings

By Robert McCloskey

"Don't you worry," said Mrs. Mallard. "I know all about bringing up children." And she did.

Boy, is that the truth. Mama Mallard didn't just send her ducklings into the big city with a wish and a prayer: She trained them how to behave properly first. She taught them to walk in a straight line behind her. She taught them how to swim and to dive. She taught them to come when called. She taught them to keep a safe distance from bikes and scooters and other wheeled objects.

It wasn't until she was satisfied with their behavior that she took them to town. Once there, did they act up? Did they run amuck, in and out of cars, panicking or being naughty?

No, they fell in line with her, "just as they had been taught."

As any woman who has been a mother more than three minutes knows, children aren't ducklings. No child I know mimics their mother with nary a fuss like the Mallard babies, but wouldn't it be nice? Much of the time, however, human babies tend to do the exact opposite of what their mothers want them to do. Want them to sit? Watch them run. Want them to go to sleep? Watch them grow more bushy-tailed by the minute.

But Mama Mallard knew instinctively what human mamas sometimes forget, that babies must be trained in the privacy and safety of home before being allowed into public lest they, in the midst of distractions and temptations, find themselves squished between two cars. Mama Mallard knew it and trained her babies accordingly.

When I was a young mama, I had no idea you could *train* children. I thought I would tell them once not to do something and they would eagerly comply. At most, I expected to repeat a lesson twice. Then, I thought (with the arrogance of the childless), that the lesson would be branded once and for all eternity into their young psyches.

My outings with Emily as a toddler proved me ever so wrong. She ran away from me in the grocery store and laughed at the end of the aisle when I couldn't catch her. She scooted away from me at Bible study. One day when I had my back turned, she ran into the street in front of our house (thankfully, it was Sunday and blessedly empty). When I took her on errands, I never knew how she would behave. She was as uncontrollable as a rogue wave, as unpredictable as Kansas weather in March, and I, the impotent bystander, watched from a distance, blood boiling, directives blissfully ignored by my deceptively innocent-looking wild child.

If only I'd known what Mama Mallard knew. That the trick to getting children to behave in public is—wait for it—getting them to behave *at home*. Training, as Mama Mallard demonstrates, puts a child in a situation, shows him what to do, then expects him to do it. If he does not do it, he is shown again what to do. If he refuses, he is given a tiny duckling sized disciplinary measure (a "dankling?") until he learns the right way. Mama Mallard did not take her uninitiated children into the city and then go berserk when they got flustered in traffic. She did not squawk at them in irritation for running around the wheels of cars or bat at them for freezing in the middle of the street.

What she did do is prepare them so that when they got into the chaos of the city, they knew exactly what to do, exactly what was expected of them. She had put them through the paces and they were ready.

One day, a few kids later and way too late for Emily, I accidentally stumbled upon a Mama Mallard trick. I was sitting on the floor eating Reeses Pieces when I called one of the kids to me. When she came to me, I gave her a candy. She was thrilled. I decided to have some fun and started to call out directives—Run to the wall! Run to me! Quick, lie down on the floor! Get up and turn around in a circle! Soon everyone wanted to "play."

They would run as fast as they could, trying to be the first to obey and would have played for hours had I not run out of candy. What a revelation. No more did mom call them to her only to remind them to be nice to each other or to stop pulling the cat's tail. Sometimes coming when mama called meant a treat or a hug. They soon learned to run to me if I so much as whispered their name.

I didn't have to use candy for long. Pretty soon, they started to associate my call with pleasure and responded faster and faster. After that, whenever obedience got sluggish, I'd pull out the Reeses and off we'd go again, a bit of a sweet refresher course to remind them of what was expected. Of course, if I had kept giving out treats to get them to come to me, I would have been in trouble. This "obeying game" is, like most tools, to be used only for a time. If overused, children come to expect a prize every time they obey and that's a game none of us wants to pull off the shelf. But sweetening obedience for a short time gets children in the habit of compliance. When the habit is established, maintenance is a breeze. It's the equivalent of getting the mossy boulder moving. Once it's in motion, it's downhill all the way and Katy bar the door.

Training a child can look any number of ways. We can play "store" and show them how to hold onto the cart and remind them not beg us for Lucky Charms. We can practice having them sit quietly on our laps. We can practice restaurant behavior at each and every meal so that going to Chili's doesn't remind some bystanding couple why they chose not to have children. Training is a dry run, a dress rehearsal. It reminds them of what is expected before it is expected. It puts them through the paces before having them run the race.

In short, it makes our (and, despite what they might think, their) lives a whole lot easier.

Thanks, Mama Mallard.

Teach Them to Fish

I'm sure you've heard the analogy before. It goes like this: You can give a person a fish (and consequently make them dependent on you for life) or you can teach them to fish (and consequently make them independent of you for life).

Mama Mallard taught her children how to fish in the literal sense, but she also taught them to fish in the figurative sense. How to cross streets without being turned into road pizza, for example. But is it reasonable to teach human children the same? After all, it's so much easier to empty the dishwasher or vacuum the stairs ourselves. If we need a job done well, can we really depend on a six-year-old to do it?

Mama Mallard would say, most emphatically, *yes*.

Teaching our children to fish is one of our primary jobs, she would argue. We need to teach them to do their own laundry, to cook, to scrape the snow off a car, and to change the oil. We need to teach them how to do dishes, how to cut up an apple, how to wash off the counters and how to unload the silverware. They need to know how to balance a checkbook and how to keep a job. They need to know how to write a thank you note, and how often to change their bed sheets. They need to understand why we stay out of debt and when a noodle is done cooking.

Some moms get a deep sense of gratification from doing these things themselves. They want to feel needed. But, having children isn't about us. It's about them. And, for all the worrying we do about our child's "self-esteem," nothing does more toward that end than helping them become independent and competent. A ten-year-old who depends on mommy to make his PB&J soon turns into a twenty-year-old who depends on mommy to pack his ham and swiss and wash his delicates in seven cold rinses. Yes, you're needed, but...ew!

Mamas can use everyday circumstances to teach their ducklings to fish. Finding a loose button on a dress coat is a perfect time to teach a boy how to sew it on properly. A girl who is having a slumber party with her friends is in a great position to learn how to make seven-layer dip. A teenager who screams at his mother to do his laundry is in a perfect position to learn to do it himself. Have a broken dryer? Have your boys look up the model on the Internet and figure out what is wrong. Need your Thanksgiving tablecloth ironed? Teach the twelve-year-old how to do it.

Mama Mallard would be the first to admit that doing it yourself is often easier. Sometimes far easier. But being a mama isn't about ease, it's about preparing our children for life. If we don't, we shouldn't be surprised if they expect us to fry them up a fish and chip supper every night.

For the rest of their lives.

The Story of Ferdinand

Written by Munro Leaf

"All the other little bulls he lived with would run and jump and butt their heads together, but not Ferdinand."

Everyone in Spain expected Ferdinand to act like the other bulls, to be fierce and to butt his head against the other bulls' heads to train for bull fighting in the arena. But Ferdinand didn't want to. He wanted to sit under his favorite cork tree.

Everyone wanted Ferdinand to fight the matador in the arena. But he didn't want to. He wanted to smell the flowers in the ladies' hair and pick the petals off daisies.

Finally, in exasperation, the trainers pulled him out of the bull-fighting circuit and took him back home.

I'm not sure, but my guess is that he's probably still there, sitting under his favorite cork tree, smelling the flowers.

ver heard of a kid like Ferdinand, a child who just didn't fit into the expected mold?

Maybe she likes staring into space rather than reading. Maybe he prefers cooking to football. Maybe she likes to work on cars. Maybe he likes spending his Saturday afternoons pinning bugs to cardboard rather than racing his friends down the street on their bikes.

As a society, we publicly honor an individual's rights to, uh, individuality. Then we bludgeon them for being unique. Why do all boys need to play football and all girls need to be cheerleaders, for example? One look around a middle school is enough to convince the bystander that standing out isn't generally met with wild approval.

What Ferdinand was wasn't morally wrong. He just didn't meet his culture's expectations. Expectation in Madrid mandated that all bulls enter the arena. They were supposed to be fierce. Tough. Nostril flaring, hoof stamping killers.

And Ferdinand wasn't.

He liked sitting under trees.

He liked flowers.

Have you ever feared you might be raising a Ferdinand? Does this frighten you down to the tips of your freshly pedicured toes?

I know of a father who took back a truck he had given his son when his son refused to play football.

I know of parents who force music lessons on children who have the musical inclination of a stone.

I know of parents who belittle (sometimes ever so subtly) their children for not being tough or aggressive enough. I know others who mock their children for not being feminine or phlegmatic enough. I myself have been guilty of, among a long litany of other things, not hiding my disappointment in one son for liking video games more than books. At various times I've wondered why one child is so laid back why another is so high strung, why one puts the Energizer Bunny to shame while another is as relaxed as Jell-O. I've often gone to bed wondering, *What is wrong with my children?*

The answer is simple: Absolutely nothing. God made everyone different, that's all. Some boys are bookish and sentimental. Some are rough-and-tumble He-Men. Some girls love dresses and dollies. Some want to drive tractors, double clutching uphill in their bare feet.

But, rather than panicking, like the bull trainers did, we can learn from Ferdinand's mother. At first she worried, yes. She thought Ferdinand might be lonely without skipping about and butting heads with the other bulls. She even questioned Ferdinand about it. But then she saw he wasn't lonely at all, and "because she was an understanding mother she just let him sit there and be happy."

Can you "just sit there" and let your child be happy, exactly as he or she is, right in the center of his/her personality? Can you accept him, love him, just as he was made? Can you be the kind of understanding mother Ferdinand's mother was?

Imagine how forcing Ferdinand to fight in the arena would have wounded his spirit. Imagine being forced to be something *you* aren't. Imagine being scoffed at for being too talkative, too quiet, too clumsy, too excitable, too singularly focused, or too imaginative. Imagine that, and then imagine a different world, one where you and your quirks and passions and personality are honored, respected, and supported, where you are loved... just as you are.

Tell me, then, do you see the wisdom in what Ferdinand's mother did or not?

I bet you do. And, if you're courageous enough to parent from that perspective, your children will rise up and call you blessed. And that's no bull.

Stone Soup

TOLD AND PICTURED BY MARCIA BROWN

"Many thanks for what you have taught us," the peasants said to the soldiers. "We shall never go hungry, now that we know how to make soup from stones."

Three soldiers on their way home from the war are perishing from hunger and enter a small village to ask for a place to rest and a bit of food. But the villagers fear they don't have enough food even for themselves, so they hide their extra food and tell the soldiers they don't have enough to share.

"Well, then," says one of the soldiers, "We'll have to make stone soup."

The villagers watch with fascination as the soldiers proceed to make a fire and place three stones in the bottom of a large iron pot filled with water.

"Any soup needs salt and pepper," one soldier says. The villagers bring salt and pepper.

"Stones like these generally make good soup. But oh, if there were carrots, it would be much better," another soldier says.

Then, one item at a time, the unsuspecting townspeople fill the pot with all sorts of wonderful things—potatoes, onions, cabbage, milk, beef. Before long, the villagers set up tables, bring out the bread and cider, and make a feast out of the "stone" soup. They dance the night away, completely unaware the soldiers have pulled one over on them.

he soldiers in *Stone Soup* were ~~manipulative~~ clever. They ~~bamboozled~~ charmed a whole village overnight. Who knew such a thing was possible with just three smooth stones?

Such a quick-witted feat was surely not easy to pull off, but, by incorporating some of the soldier's ~~tricks~~ wisdom, we, too, can get our little villagers at home to work together like a well-oiled tricycle. That is what this simple, yet profound, story is all about—working together. So, the next time we need the garden weeded or the basement organized, perhaps we should listen to what the soldiers might tell us, if they were here today:

"Mama troops, listen up! Want to get your subordinates to work without complaint? Then do what we did…

1. Pique their curiosity—*Nothing "works" better than making someone believe something is their own idea. Come up with the equivalent of, "Well then, we'll just have to make stone soup," but tailor it for whatever project you need done. Kids balk at weeding the garden? "Hmmm, I wonder what we could make with these raspberries and strawberries?" (Smoothies!) Kids don't want to clean the garage? "Hmmm, I wonder what we could do with that half of the garage if it wasn't full of junk?" (Make a workbench for the boys to build swords on!) Basement filled to the rafters? "Hmmm, too bad there's not enough room cleared out for a fort down here."*

You get the idea.

2. Ask for and accept input—*If you are micromanaging every detail of a big project, insisting it be done your way and your way only, expect resistance. Just like we didn't control what went into the villagers' soup, don't control or limit the ways in which your children can help. Ask your daughter how she thinks the living room might be better arranged. If you have the tools on one side of the garage and the boys say they could find them better if they were on a different side, consider moving the tools. Does the lawn need to be mowed from the curb to the front porch or can you allow your artistic son to mow it diagonally or like a checkerboard or in the shape of George Washington's face?*

3. Make it enjoyable—*Turn on Michael Jackson or the* Glee *soundtrack. Strike up a riveting conversation. Bring out cold Cokes. Go pick up dollar hamburgers. Work does not need to be drudgerous. Repeat that sentence three times and then tattoo it on your forehead. Cider and feasting, remember?*

4. Many hands make light work—*Instead of sending the kids into all four corners of the house on cleaning day to "be efficient," work together as much as possible. There is no reason children can't help with dishes, gardening, plant watering, flower planting, porch sweeping, bathroom cleaning, cabinet reorganizing, car cleaning, deck building, basement finishing, or painting, especially if you are working side by side. Bonus: Work getting done sooner = More time to play.*

5. Reap the benefits of working together—*If we had made the soup by ourselves, instead of incorporating the community into the project, our evening would probably not have ended in a party. When you do a job by yourselves, parents,* *you rob your children of time you could have spent together, of feeling good about a job done well, of a chance to teach them new skills, and of being a contributing member of the family. In other words, parents who send Susie to get ready for bed while they clean up the kitchen are missing out on a chance to talk to her about her day. Parents who shoo Jonny off to the TV while they wash the cars are overlooking the perfect opportunity to train him how to to do it himself.*

Got it? Carry on, soldiers!"

Thanks, guys. You confirm what I've suspected for a long time.

When we share the work, we are giving our children ownership in the final result. This builds in them both competence and confidence. Working together is a great time to build memories (my kids fondly remember weeding our one-acre yard in Colorado, right, kids? Kids?) Just like the soldiers and the villagers discovered, people who work together also get to celebrate together. When we finished remodeling our basement together several years ago, we felt a joint sense of pride in our new rooms. We now fondly reminisce about various disasters that befell us while work was in progress like the time we stayed up half the night painting the living room only to realize the next day that we had painted the room a different shade of tan from the rest of the house.

See? Happy, happy times. And they can be yours, too, if only you imitate the ways of the *Stone Soup* soldiers. And, if you're discreet about it, your kids won't know how they ended up re-wallpapering the kitchen at three in the morning, they'll just know they had a blast doing it.

Green Eggs and Ham

By Dr. Seuss

"I do not like green eggs and ham! I do not like them, Sam-I-am."

Sam-I-Am is a persistent little cuss. Even after chasing the nameless main character (whom we will call the Green Egg guy) into a house with a mouse and into a box with a fox and onto a boat with a goat, Sam just can't get him to try green eggs and ham. But does this stop him? No. He continues to hound the Green Egg guy until, just to shut him up, the Green Egg guy agrees to try them. And, guess what? Despite adamantly claiming he hated green eggs and ham, it turns out he likes them so much that he would indeed eat them on a boat and with a goat, in a car or on a train, in the dark and in the rain…in fact, he'd eat them anywhere!

"Try it, you'll like it," was a phrase my mother used whenever she served horrid foods like okra, cauliflower, or Brussels sprouts. She repeated it so often that, even though my father was a pastor and I ought to have known better, I thought it was a Bible verse. I loved Jesus and tried hard to obey Him, but when it came to cooked vegetables, I had to sin so that grace could abound. My parents would find peas lined up on the stairs and squishy foods spit into my napkin. I just couldn't eat them. But that didn't stop them from making me. Childhood meals often ended with me still at the table, facing a huge bowl of some lukewarm vegetable and the words, "You'll sit here until you finish it," ringing in my ears.

My parents weren't tyrants. They were simply teaching me what they were taught—to eat what's put in front of you no matter how disgusting it is. Waste not, want not, there are children starving in Africa, and so on and so forth.

Sam-I-Am must have been raised by parents like mine. He doggedly pursues the Green Egg guy, thrusting a plate of green eggs and ham in front of him at every opportunity in his attempt to get him to try it and like it. He doesn't accept no for an answer.

And, to some extent, it works. To shut Sam up, our guy finally does try the eggs and ham and, yes, he realizes he likes them, which proves that the method works, right?

Wrong.

Successful as Sam appears at first blush, I doubt he and the Green Egg guy get their families together for summer barbecues or play golf together on the weekends. Pushing our wills onto other people, like Sam does to the Green Egg guy, doesn't make for good long-term relationships, even if those relationships are with people who happen to be under three feet tall and call us "Mommy."

Children are born with a God-given sense of personhood. They have preferences just like adults do and, unless we want the resistance Sam got, (within reason) we ought to honor those preferences. *Of course*, most of growing up is about doing what others tell us to do. Parents are in charge, after all, and in no way am I advocating we give our kids endless choices or bow to their every whim. None of us want to raise demigods who are above the fifth commandment. I'm simply saying that children need it to be okay to sometimes say no, I'm not comfortable with that, or I'd rather not, or Thank you, but no, or I'd rather have some salad than those horrendous peas.

When kids (especially older ones) get their personhood stepped on, they might resist not because they're rebelling, but because we've gone about it the wrong way. We've engaged with them on a personhood level, drawn an arbitrary line in the sand, and now their personhood demands they dig in their heels. It reminds me of the time my parents told my sister, Joanna, to eat her scrambled eggs. She did, and they were still in her mouth when we got home from church four hours later. Personhood was at stake.

Sam-I-Am parenting smothers a child because it allows no room for personhood. It works, but at a price. Sam-I-Am parenting is one of the storybook examples of what parents ought *not* to do.

So, with deepest apologies to dear Dr. Seuss, I offer a different, albeit less rhyming, approach to getting the Green Egg guy to eat the eggs and ham.

Imagine this:

Sam-I-Am comes in riding his dog, introduces himself, and asks the Green Egg guy if he wants some green eggs and ham. The Green Egg guy says, politely, "No, thank you, I do not like green eggs and ham." Whereupon Sam sets them on a table in front of him and says, "Oh, have you tried them?" Our guy says no, he has not. "Hmm," says Sam. "I used to not like them either. But they're actually quite tasty. No pressure, though. I'll leave them here for awhile because I've got some more dog riding to do, but I'll be back in a bit to pick them up."

With the heat off and his personhood intact, my guess is, once Sam's back is turned, our Green Egg guy may very well give those eggs a chance.

Because even though "Try it, you'll like it" isn't found anywhere in the canon of Scripture, it really is a good policy. We just can't Sam-I-Am our way into getting our kids to do it.

Mike Mulligan and His Steam Shovel

Story and Pictures by Virginia Lee Burton

"Never had Mike Mulligan and Mary Anne had so many people to watch them; never had they dug so fast and so well…"

Mike Mulligan and his faithful steam engine, Mary Anne, loved to work. Or they did until the diesel engines and the gas engines put them out of business. This made them VERY SAD. But then they found out that the town of Popperville needed someone to dig a basement for their new City Hall. Knowing the odds were against them getting the job, Mike tells the city that he and Mary Anne will dig that cellar before the sun goes down or they won't have to pay a cent. Henry B. Swap, one of the city's selectmen, confident that it would take a hundred men to do the job, sees a free cellar in his future, so heartily agrees.

As the clock starts ticking, Mike tells a young boy to watch them work because they "always dig better and faster if someone is watching." The boy goes and finds as many people as he can to watch and, sure enough, Mike and Mary Anne dig better and faster than they ever have before, finishing the last corner of the basement just as the sun goes down.

ust like Mike and Mary Anne, I work better when someone is watching me, don't you? But not just any old someone, an encouraging someone, like the little boy who cheered on Mike and Mary Anne. His faith could very well be what propelled the two of them to work "better and faster" than they had ever worked before. Today we know the name for what he and the other bystanders were to Mike and Mary Anne: Good Finders.

To properly envision the power of Good Finding, first imagine it's opposite: What if crotchety old Henry B. Swap, who secretly wanted Mike to fail so he could get the basement dug for free, had been the only one watching that day?

"Oh, Mike, I know you, you lazy good-for-nothing. You'll never get this done in time. You and that outdated wreck'o metal call your rusted selves professionals? Three days, maybe five, but never just one. I'd bet my hat you don't get half of it done before nightfall."

Who knows, with words like that ringing in his ears, Mike might never have had a book written about him.

Instead, Mike defies the naysayers, including mean old Mr. Swap.

Mamas, we need to be Good-Finders like that boy was to Mike, constantly on the lookout for what is good in our children.

But beware: Kids aren't stupid. They know when we're being genuine and when we're praising them simply because some "expert" thirty years ago said we should. False praise is contrived, reaching, and intended to give our children props for meeting minimum expectations: Thanking them profusely for eating their broccoli. Gushing over half-hearted school work. Tripping over ourselves to bandaid their spirits when life kicks them ever so gently in the teeth.

No one, least of all our children, is fooled by that.

Genuine praise, on the other hand, is tied to actual accomplishment or effort. "Honey, thank you for emptying the trash tonight. I was tired and it was so nice to walk in and see it already done for me." "Hey, the kitchen looks *great* today. You worked hard. Thanks, love."

We don't need to dream up ways to plump up our children's self-esteem. We only need to be like that little boy watching Mike and Mary Anne, benevolently watching for opportunities to be their cheerleaders and encouraging them with abandon when the occasion arises.

Do this and watch their cellars be excavated, all four corners dug straight down in a single day.

The Mitten

UKRAINIAN FOLK TALE, ADAPTED & ILLUSTRATED BY JAN BRETT

"The little mitten was getting crowded."

Have you ever felt stretched so thin you thought you might break?
That's how the mitten in this story must have felt as first a mole, then a rabbit, a hedgehog, an owl, a badger, a fox, and, finally, a giant bear crammed their hairy, feathery, prickly, or furry bodies into its hand-knitted self.

Can you imagine what she must have been thinking by the time the fox came along?

"You've got to be joking.

I mean, here I was nice enough to let that little mole in to get warm. It IS colder than an Eskimo skating party out there. And, although it didn't feel very good, when the rabbit came by wanting a place to snuggle, I did my best to accommodate both him and his ears.

But, the hedgehog? His prickles snagged my lovely knitted sides and, I think, may have snipped right through my thumb. As if that wasn't enough, the owl swaggered over with this sense of entitlement, as though I have nothing better to do but put up with his sharp talons and bird breath. But at least he stayed quiet, whereas the badger sauntered in rear-end first and started chatting away ad infinitum. And the fox? Well, I can hardly describe what it felt like to have that fur ball wedging his way in.

One word: Bath time.

By the time he was curled up next to the others, I had had it! Calgon, please, take me away. Better yet, take *them* away. Do other mittens have to put up with this kind of treatment? I don't hear any thank yous in there, people. Doesn't anyone in there care about me? I will never look, much less *feel*, the same after this. My left hand mate will always, do you hear me, ALWAYS rub in how wide my hips are compared to hers.

Listen to me, people. I can't take another thing. I've had it up to here with the lot of you. GET. OUT!"

Stretched beyond her limits, the irony is that it isn't the huge bear that does her in. It's a teensy mouse, no bigger than her knitted thumb. His tiny tail tickles the bear's nose and poof! Out everyone flies, leaving nothing but the stretched-out mitten floating in the winter sky. Even though she had borne the burden of having seven animals stuffed inside her yarny self, the diminutive mouse was the last straw.

Poor mitten.

e talk about the straw that breaks the camel's back, but what we don't know is why something as light as straw is able to crush through bone. I would like to suggest that the straw isn't, in fact, what breaks the camel's back. The straw is just who got blamed, the last remembered event before we lost it. The cup of coffee we spilled on our freshly ironed skirt. The car door that banged against our shin. The key that, for some reason, won't unlock the door before the fifteenth try.

Long before it settled itself mid-vertebrae, however, that straw was just a nearly-imperceptible fiber. That first fiber might be something as innocuous as getting up fifteen minutes late. The second fiber might be realizing, halfway to work, that you are almost out of fuel. The third fiber might be spilling gas on your shoes when you go to fill up. All day long, fibers continue to build, which is why, that evening, you bite your husband's head off for missing a few crumbs while wiping off the kitchen counter. It is the proverbial 'last straw,' but we know it was far more than that—the cumulative effect of the approximately 25 fibers that had been gathering all day long.

The question the Mitten needed to ask herself wasn't "Why did I fall apart just because the mouse tickled the bear's nose?" but "Why did I give so many animals refuge in the first place?" Similarly, when we mamas fall apart, rather than asking what the final straw was, perhaps the better question to ask is what tiny fibers were quietly accumulating to form a piece of straw that was strong enough to "break" our backs.

For the Mitten, the field mouse on the bear's nose wasn't the whole straw, she was only the last fiber of the straw that tipped it into the back-breaking category.

Mamas, we need to be aware of the fibers that add up to straws that can break us. Here are a few such fibers that can add up over time:

Being tired. Being sick. Having sick children. Having an

erratic schedule. Having a husband who works long hours or who is often out of town. Unemployment. Tight finances. A child in crisis. A broken dishwasher. A discouraging Facebook comment. A saggy mattress.

Being the strong women we are, mamas usually hold up pretty well despite enduring one or two or five of these.

So we're surprised when a stubbed toe or a dirty kitchen does us in.

Understanding what is happening helps. When I cry easily, I know something is afoot, that the fibers are building up. When I snap at my kids, I know I'm nearing a straw. When I can't believe no one complimented my chicken Alfredo, I know the chicken isn't the issue.

The Mitten's plight teaches us to take notice of the microscopic fibers that eventually form straws that can wreak havoc on our spines and our lives. In retrospect, I'm sure even the mitten would admit that she should have established some boundaries. Only furry creatures allowed. Birds on Mondays, Wednesdays, and Fridays. Bears can visit, but only *by themselves.*

Mamas can take the same kind of preventative measures. Exhaustion makes you say four-letter words in front of the kids? Beg, borrow, or steal more sleep. Financial pressure makes you unfit to live with? Take extra good care of yourself come bill-paying day. Husband going out of town? Wait to renovate the bathroom. Hormones flaring? Don't invite a houseful of preschoolers over.

So much of mothering is knowing our limits and setting protective boundaries around them. In other words, we should do what the Mitten *didn't:* Pay attention to the micro-fibers, learn to say no, and notice when we're feeling overstretched.

Maybe if we do, we can keep the straw in the field, in the barn, in the haystack, in the horse's feeding trough, anywhere but on our backs.

Ten Commandments for Mama-Care

1. Thou shalt take care of thy body, mind, and soul so thou doest not snap when thy toddler tinkleth on thy new rug for the twentieth time since eight in the am.

2. Thou shalt not listen to the guilt-tripping of other mothers, even and especially those claiming to hold The Corner on Truth.

3. Thou shalt take plenty of long luxurious baths.

4. Thou shalt exercise so thy body is strong, even if it means doing push ups on the staircase, power lifting the baby, and jogging in place during *Veggie Tales*.

5. Thou shalt read and groweth thy mind lest thou become a boring ignoramus.

6. Thou shalt find thy Ya-Ya's and bringeth them hot soups when they are in need. In return, thou shalt receive hot soups when thou art in need, even, and especially, if thou pridest thyself on never needing anything from anyone, *ever*.

7. Thou shalt trust thy gut.

8. Thou shalt not complain longer than three minutes. Talk fast.

9. Thou shalt not resent thy children, even when they commence to throw up the night before thou art to depart for Maui.

10. Thou shalt honor Date Night and keep it sacred. Remember the Date Night and sanctify it. Thou shalt not talk about potty training and spit-up whilst on Date Night. Thou shalt not fuss at thy respective mate for his or her myriad of deficiencies on Date Night. On Date Night thou shalt kiss him upon the lips and laugh at his jokes and end the night in his hairy, yet surprisingly still sexy, arms.

Olivia

By Ian Falconer

"This is Olivia. She is good at lots of things. She is *very* good at wearing people out."

If you haven't yet met the imaginative Olivia, I highly suggest it. But you might want to drink a cup of coffee or take your multivitamin first because Olivia's boundless energy is going to wear you out.

At times, she wears her own self out.

For one thing, she changes clothes about twenty times a day. She plays overachiever at the beach during sand castle construction time. She dances during "naps." She attempts to copy famous paintings… on her bedroom wall. She negotiates the number of bedtime stories she wants her mother to read with the skill of a trial lawyer.

Finally, Olivia goes to bed. Ah, peace at last. But no. She is now dreaming about being an opera star, dressed to the nines, singing on stage. Not even sleep can rescue Olivia from her wild and whimsical imagination.

aybe it's because I'm hopelessly sentimental, but Olivia makes me miss my own childhood.

In those days (not *that* long ago, mind you), children were given two choices: Use your imagination or die of boredom.

These days, except for kids like Olivia, kids are rarely bored enough to engage their imaginations. And it's a wretched shame.

Perhaps it's because we live in Kansas, where summer temperatures vacillate between Molten Lava and Lucifer's Abode, but, once school is out, the school playground across the street and the forest beyond are many times empty. I don't often see kids on their bikes or catching fish in the creek or flying kites.

When I was growing up in Washington State, my mother would threaten us with a list of jobs she procured from a gulag somewhere if we set so much as a toenail inside the house between the months of June and September. With months of hot summer hours to kill outside, we had no choice but to be creative. We built a go-kart out of an old pallet and pushed each other around the neighborhood. We played baseball in our cul-de-sac. We tried to sell ash from Mt. St. Helens to the neighbors. We stalked Big Foot. We tried to get to Narnia.

It was fabulous. And it makes me wonder, like Mary Higgins Clark, *Where are the children?*

If you have any older than the age of three, you know the answer to that question: They're plugged in. They're in front of televisions, computers, video games, iPads, iTouches, iPods, iPhones, Game Boys, and Nintendo DS's, plugged in and tuned out. Antiquated activities like conversation and book reading are going the way of the cassette tape and the VCR. Kids are too busy checking email, Facebooking, Skyping, or texting to put any effort into that silly imagination business.

Long, boring road trips are no oasis from the imaginative desert created by technology. It's not uncommon to drive by a mini-van and see several children parked in front of three or four portable DVD players, each with his own earbuds, watching his or her movie of choice. Mom is on her Kindle Fire playing Words With Friends and dad is listening to the John Grisham novel he downloaded from Audible.com. It is perfectly—and eerily—silent. Goodbye license plate game. Goodbye, "How many more miiiiiiiiles???" Goodbye "99 Bottles of Beer on the Wall."

Whatever happened to blanket forts and championship Monopoly games and homemade play dough? Whatever happened to summer night bubble baths in the wading pool? Whatever happened to finger painting and tree climbing and giggling in a bean bag chair together?

Screen time is the techno-equivalent of feeding children candy instead of fruit. It is simply too yummy to resist. And I'm not talking about just for the children. Because, here's the kicker: A plugged-in child is a quiet child. What crazy parent would *purposely turn off the TV* when doing so means having to provide other entertainment options like reading, going to the park, cookie baking, or riding bikes together? Those activities are loud and messy and time-consuming. Blech!

As much as I fuss about technology, it isn't going anywhere. In its place, it has many benefits as any of you with iPhones well know. So, what is a parent to do?

Honestly, I'm not sure. If you have more than 1.3 children, monitoring screen time quickly makes mom a prison warden. Bribing children with a certain amount of computer time for every book read works for some parents. Establishing technology-free zones like Sundays and evenings between four and eight works for others. Banning computers altogether works for a dwindling few.

Moms' biggest challenge in the age of instant entertainment is finding ways to let her little critters get bored. And often this means unplugging them. But be forewarned, mamas: It's gonna hurt. Coming off the dopamine high of video games or waking up from the sleepy beta mode of television hurts more than frostbitten skin coming back to life. That our children will buck our efforts is as sure as the setting of the sun. They won't like it any more than they do when we ration out their Halloween candy over the course of a month. But it's just as good for them.

Instead of clamping down even harder on screen time, perhaps our efforts should be directed toward making non-screen life more enticing. Because, for a child to pick something "harder" like Boggle over something "easier" like Fruit Ninja, that "harder" thing has got to be far more appealing than the "easier" thing. We might even have to (gulp) *do something with them.*

Perhaps we should ask Olivia's mother, who seems to have this imagination stuff down pat, what her trick is. Because the whirlwind of a girl she raised seems to have no trouble whatsoever in this area.

My guess is, she just let her get good and bored.

The Giving Tree

BY SHEL SILVERSTEIN

"And the tree was happy...but not really."

The Giving Tree *is about a tree and a boy who grow up together. The boy makes the tree's leaves into crowns. The tree lets him climb up her trunk. He swings from her branches, eats her apples, plays hide-and-go-seek with her, and sleeps in her shade. She loves him and he loves her.*

But the boy grows up into a young man who outgrows his need to play with the tree. What he wants, he says, is money. That will make him happy. So the tree gives him her apples to sell and make money and this makes them both happy...for awhile.

The boy grows a little older and, although he is too busy to climb up the tree's trunk, he is very *interested in a house. Can the tree give him a house? No, she says, but she can give him her branches to make a house. She wants him to be happy.*

The tree continues to give and give and give, hoping it will make the boy happy. Giving to him makes her happy, or so she says.

Finally, the boy visits the tree one last time. She's given so much that there is nothing but a stump left to her and the boy is now an old man. She is sorry she has nothing left to give him, she sighs. He has no teeth to eat her apples with anyway, he sighs. So she offers him the only thing she has left, a seat for him to rest his weary bones on.

He accepts...and she is happy.

r is she?

The first time I heard of *The Giving Tree* I was sitting in the book section of Target with a friend who was crying as she read it to me. The tree was so sacrificial (sob), so selfless (sob), so… giving (huge sob). Wasn't I moved?

Call me a cynic, but the only thing that threatened to move me to tears was how insufferably selfish the boy was to take advantage of the tree's generosity like that. Is this the sort of sacrificial love people, specifically mothers, are supposed to shoot for?

Well, yes…and no. Of course we want to give to our children. We would happily lay our lives down for them and do, in hundreds of ways throughout their lives. But this isn't what is implied in *The Giving Tree*. What is implied is that we should give and give and give until there is nothing left of us, but a dried-up stump. Oh, and ungrateful, self-centered adult children to remind us of our failings.

Most children don't praise their parents for all they do. They take what we do for granted. The more a parent does for a child, the more the child expects can and will be done for him. The parent who does everything, or nearly everything, for her child in lieu of taking care of herself is not doing her child any favor. She may feel nurturing and kind towards him, but if she fills all the gaps, pours every glass of milk, and covers all his bases, she is neither preparing him for the real world nor modeling for him how one person can love another while still taking care of themselves.

Sadly, what she can therefore expect, rather than a long string of mushy Mother's Day cards, is a child (and eventually an adult) who is demanding and nearly impossible to please. He doesn't appreciate her because she didn't appreciate herself enough to expect him to. He doesn't offer to help her because he was always on the receiving end of such offerings. He does not fend for himself because he's always leaned on mama and she was all too happy to let him. He, like the boy in the story, only takes more and more and more until she is nothing but a worn-out stump. Perhaps, if she is lucky, her child may come to her on her death bed to finally acknowledge her sacrifice, but don't count on it. The rather dismal future she has to look forward to has been built through the most innocent of actions, the most demure of well-intended choices. Who would think that *giving* could create a monster?

I hate to step on the toes of any of you who, like my friend, love this book. But when we're looking at what *The Giving Tree* implies for mamas, we have to acknowledge it isn't a pretty picture. The boy in the book can be construed in no other way than selfish and self-absorbed. If that's the kind of child you don't mind raising, by all means give away. However, if you want your child to grow up and truly appreciate you (and all the other people in his life), love him, support him, and encourage him. But, whatever you do, don't cut off your limbs for him.

When I was a young mama, well-meaning friends encouraged me to be limbless, which meant never doing anything "selfish" like reading a book over lunch or going to bed early. I was supposed to do only those things deemed sacrificial.

So I did. I spent my lunches asking my children stimulating questions and, on the rare occasion I did divert my attention from them for a few, guilty moments in order to, say, clean myself, it was only for an abbreviated shower. For the longest time I did nothing "for myself" and questioned every activity I was involved in to root out any seed of selfishness. Because, as I was taught, taking care of yourself is a major mommy no-no. Taking care of myself meant I cared for myself more than my family. It meant I was riddled with narcissism. It meant I probably should have never procreated in the first place.

Not that I can blame it all on my friends. As I tend to do in many areas of my life, I took it too far. I was always on some extreme eating plan. No fat this week. No carbs the next. No sugar. No caffeine. No treats. No junk. No citrus. Nothing white. Nothing flavorful. Nothing that made me happy. I felt so guilty about owning white sugar (for emergency purposes only, of course) that I hid the container under the counter so my friends wouldn't see it when they visited. I baked with molasses and substituted applesauce for butter in my baking recipes. I mowed the yard before breakfast and spent the children's nap times doing something "worthy" and "constructive" like making paper chains to count down the days to Christmas or folding their panties into perfect squares.

And I was miserable.

Of course, you probably don't do silly things like I did, but maybe you have your own list of "selfish" behaviors you have long tried to eradicate: Sleeping in until seven. Reading instead of teaching your children poetry. Arranging play dates for "them." Hiding Hostess cherry pies in the back of the cabinet where they can't see or reach them. Exercising.

Seriously, here's a news flash, Miss Giving Tree: Ignoring your own needs isn't selfless, but the exact opposite. Being exhausted and strung out and hungry and intellectually deprived does not a good mother make. It does, however, a good *martyr* make. A martyr who complains ad infinitum about how busy she is and how tired and how worn out and how overdone and how neglected and how under appreciated, as she grasps for sympathy. But, even though *mother* eerily rhymes with *martyr,* a wise mama will avoid likening the two and instead, like they tell us on the airplane, put on her own mask first.

Because oxygen is essential for life. And if mama is getting enough of it (and sleep and joy and good Indian food), chances are, she'll have some (apples to eat, branches to play on, trunks to climb) to give everyone else.

The Velveteen Rabbit

By Margery Williams

"Real isn't how you are made," said the Skin Horse. "It's a thing that happens to you."

In the beloved children's story, The Velveteen Rabbit, *the Boy's stuffed Rabbit learns that Being Real is what happens when a child really, truly loves you. It sometimes hurts and it doesn't happen all at once. Being real is a process. "You become," says the wise Skin Horse. "It takes a long time. That's why it doesn't often happen to people who break easily, or have sharp edges, or who have to be carefully kept." The Velveteen Rabbit eventually learns that even though becoming real isn't easy, it's the best way to be.*

I remember the day I figured out my mother was real.

For some reason, she was sad and sat crying in her 1970s gold tweed rocking chair. My siblings and I had never seen Mom cry before, so this was a Big Deal. We figured Dad was dead or that we had run out of money and were being sent to the orphanage like Annie or Oliver Twist. So I and my four younger siblings, gathered around Mom, one of us on each arm of the chair, two on its back, and one in her lap. None of us except Mom knew why, but we all rocked, we all cried. Then, without warning, the chair keeled over backwards, dumping all six of us onto the floor.

Tears turned to laughter as we picked ourselves up, rubbed our heads, and uprighted the chair. Mom told us that Dad was still living and we still had a little money, so weren't quite at the point of calling the orphanage just yet. Our laughter was all the sweeter because we were so very, very relieved that even though Mom cried, life was still going to go on.

That's an important lesson for children to learn. That moms and dads are human. That they have good days and that they have rotten days. That they get sick and feel tired and get in fights with each other and with their friends, just like kids do. That they can cry and life will go on.

Showing our kids we are real doesn't mean we have to bend over backwards to fall apart in their presence. Do that too much and they might 411 the local insane asylum. But guarding them from every human and natural response to life's struggles is not doing them any favor. They need to see us face discouragement so they know how to handle it themselves when discouragement finds them one day. They need to see us fall apart so that they know how to get themselves back together again when they fall apart. By allowing them to see us in a myriad of emotional states, we are imprinting authenticity on their very souls.

I know of a man and woman whose relationship seemed so perfect they became our church's model couple. All of us looked up to them even more when they admitted, during a Valentine's Day banquet, that never once in thirty years had they raised their voices at each other. Wow, we all thought, that's a marriage!

But the thrill didn't last. Later, I discovered that most of the couples at the banquet found the couple's admission disheartening. Because, while this couple's relationship was admirable, it wasn't imitable. All of us in the room had already yelled at our spouses. It made me strangely glad for the fights my parents had, because when I got married I thought, We got through a *whole day* without fighting, we must have the best marriage ever! They gave me a perfect example of imperfect authenticity and, as an adult, I am most grateful for it.

In *The Velveteen Rabbit*, the Boy's crushed velvet rabbit becomes Real only when, in his passionate love for it, the boy rubs all the fur off its ears. Isn't it wonderful to know that when you are real, your children will love you even more? Our imperfect moments show our children how to recover from life's curveballs. It is how the fur is rubbed off our ears. *The Velveteen Rabbit* teaches us not to duct tape ourselves together to appear like flawless marionettes, nor to hide every hint of humanity from our families. A tear here, a little frustration there can show our kids not only that we are human, but that humans survive hard times. They come, yes, but they usually don't last. Being Real means we're not just mimes behind white makeup or clowns behind bulbous red noses. We're flesh and blood, fallible, and as sensitive to criticism as the next guy. Being Real allows our children to step outside their own troubles and see the troubles of someone else. It helps grow empathy in them. If we put on the happy face and the "I'm fine" facade the whole time our kids are growing up, how will they ever know that having some fur rubbed off their ears is the sign of a life well-lived, that being tattered around the edges means they've truly lived and truly been loved? How will they ever know what it means to Be Real?

The Saggy Baggy Elephant

By Kathryn and Byron Jackson

"I'd better hide in a dark place where my bags and sags and wrinkles won't show."

Sooki the elephant was dancing around the jungle happy as can be with a one-two-three-kick that shook the trees and pounded the ground. He thought his dancing was great until a snotty parrot stopped him in his tracks.

"Why are you shaking the jungle all to pieces," he cried. "What kind of animal are you anyway?"

Well, that got Sooki to thinking, because actually he didn't know what kind of animal he was. All he knew is that no one in the jungle looked saggy and baggy like he did.

"I dance and I kick—and I call myself Sooki. It's a good-sounding name, and it fits me, don't you think?"

"'Maybe," answered the parrot, "but if it does, it's the only thing that does fit you. Your ears are too big for you, and your nose is way too big for you. And your skin is much, MUCH too big for you. It's baggy and saggy. You should call yourself Saggy-Baggy!"'

Sooki, now aware of his many flaws and suddenly self-conscious, tries everything to get rid of his sags and bags, rubbing his skin with his trunk, pulling up his pant legs, soaking in water, and exercising.

It wasn't until a lion threatened to turn him into dinner that he trumpeted as loudly as he could and, what do you know, a whole herd of elephants just like him, answered his call and came to his rescue. He thought they were beautiful.

"*I wish I looked just like you,*" *he said.*

"*You do,*" *they replied.* "*You're a perfectly dandy little elephant!*"

Do you love your body?

I'm not asking if you love it like you love your baby's dimpled thighs or the fat on the back of his neck, but do you accept it for what it is?

Yeah, me neither.

Just like Sooki, I look in the mirror and see one flaw after the other. Some parts sag. Some parts lag. Some are getting wrinkled. Some—wild horses won't drag out *which*—have shrunk. Lines are appearing. Sun spots are showing up. Plus, I have these fat blobs that poke out between my arm and my chest that no amount of exercise eradicates. In fact, every push-up makes them stick out, yup, *further*.

Like my body? I wouldn't exactly put it that way.

Tolerate under protest, maybe…on a good day.

Wouldn't it be great if one day you were whisked away to a planet full of people who had your same exact body composition? Everyone had your apple build with chicken legs. Your thick neck. Your flat, but wide rear end. For once, you fit in, felt like you belonged, and didn't worry about not looking any other way because *no one* looked any other way. You didn't envy someone else's tiny frame or her long, lanky legs because you didn't know such things existed.

That's how the Sooki must have felt when he found his herd. Can you imagine his relief in knowing that his saggy, baggy skin was no mistake, that it was how he was made, that he was beautiful and wondrous, just as he was?

I see this no more clearly than in my three daughters. They each struggle with "bags" of their own. One thinks she has too many freckles. One wishes for longer legs. One abhors her prickly skin. Yet, when I look at them, I just see *them*. Their sweet natures. Their fire. Their kindness. Their passion. I don't look at one and say, oh gosh, there goes Miss Prickle Arms again or gee, she'd be so much cuter if her legs were of a decent length. I think of some friends who have five daughters. Some are brunettes, some are blonde, some have curls, some don't, some have blue eyes, some have brown, some are funny, some well-spoken, some quiet, all of them cuddly. Each one is unique in her own right, making it impossible to pick a "favorite" among the bunch. I hate the thought of any of these girls not being comfortable in her skin, because each one radiates a beauty all her own.

As we all do. Beauty is (or should be) subjective. A good looking woman who is a spoiled wench isn't beautiful. A plain woman whose eyes shine from the depths of her bright spirit *is*. Those who are brave enough to buck trends, dress originally, and play with color and texture can make a Gap model look trite and one-dimensional.

This vignette started out talking about fitting in and now it's ending by talking about standing out. But maybe it's okay just this once to break a writing rule and not bookend it with perfect parallelity. Because sometimes we have to know how we fit in before we have the courage to stand out. The Saggy Baggy Elephant was lost, searching for an explanation for his baggy skin, unsure of how he looked until he found a herd of creatures just like him. He was so happy to find out that he was perfectly fine just as he was, 'that he began to dance one-two-three-kick through the jungle.'

And what happened, you ask, to the parrot who had done his best to instill insecurity in sweet Sooki?

"…This time, he didn't laugh, not even to himself."

We're Going on a Bear Hunt
By Michael Rosen

"We're going on a bear hunt. We're going to catch a big one. What a beautiful day!"

In Michael Rosen's retelling of this famous camp song, a father and his four children are trying to go on a bear hunt, but all sorts of things are in their way—long, wavy grass; a deep, cold river; thick, oozy mud; a big, dark forest; a swirling, whirling snowstorm; a narrow, gloomy cave. They have no choice: In order to find the bear, they must go through these. Thus, the repeated chorus, "We can't go over it. We can't go under it. Oh no! We've got to go through it!"

f that doesn't sound like a mantra for mamas, I'm not sure what does, for rarely can we motherly types get around certain unpleasant situations.

But at times, oh how I wish I could. I'd skip right over flu bugs and chicken pox. I'd sail by teething and potty training and coast past—waaaay past—teaching my children to drive.

But that's rarely possible. Most of the time, like the family in this story, we just have to go through it. We have to wait for the test results. We have to sit in the doctor's offices with a hundred questions and a thousand worries. We have to take our child to get blood drawn. We have to brace ourselves for potentially bad news. We have to sit up with a sick child. All. Night. Long. We have to run the shower with hot water and hope the coughing stops. We have to sit and watch teeth get pulled. We have to watch gashes stitched.

As much as we would love to stuff cotton in our ears, shove our heads in the sand, or otherwise ignore reality from time to time, the show must go on. No mom I know loves taking her children for shots or for a strep test. No mom I know loves cleaning up vomit. These are just some of the things we must go through as parents because there's simply no way around them.

I struggle with this because I'm a germ freak and a body fluid hater. There are many, many times I would pay cold hard cash to get out of some dirty task. But at our income level, I can't. And, truth is, my children need *me*, not some hired hand during times like this. In the end, it comes down to that: Their needs *must* trump my fear/discomfort/pain/exhaustion/paranoid OCD germophobia each and every time.

It's called being a mom. It's scary and tiring and messy and comfort-zone-extracting.

...and sometimes we just gotta go through it.

* * *

P.S. You didn't think I was going to leave you hanging, did you? Because, although there are times we simply *must* go through hard things with our kids, we mamas have a few tricks that make the process less painful. Emergency kits are one such trick that help us 'go through' it:

Baby/Toddler/Teenager-Is-Sick Kit: Pedialyte, Tylenol, liquid dispensers that haven't had all the dosage lines worn off yet, rags, Lysol, carpet cleaner, a collection of cute plastic buckets (might as well try to enjoy the experience), a bottle of ginger ale, the doctor's phone number written in big black letters so you can read it when it's the middle of the night or when you've been crying, a new DVD the kids haven't seen before, a new DVD *you* haven't seen before, something diverting (a new rattle for baby, a new book that makes noises for a toddler), Clorox wipes, paper towels, extra garbage can liners.

Mama-Is-Sick Kit: Those expensive lotion-loaded tissues you can't afford for the whole family. One of those microwavable neck warmers. Ibuprofen. Nyquil. Those copies of *Real Simple* you haven't had time to read yet. A new book you are dying (not literally, I hope) to read. Chamomile tea. Bath bubbles. Jane Austen anything. Chapstick.

We-Are-At-Someone-Who-Doesn't-Have-Small-Children's House: Coloring books and colored pencils (people without kids panic when kids pull out markers). I recommend the creamy and dreamy Prismacolor pencils, which cost more than Solomon's Temple, but are well worth the investment. A book on tape, CD, or iPod, depending on your level of techno-savviness. Blankie or special animal. Face/hand wipes (kids are more lovable when they're not disgusting). A cup with a Ft.

Knox of a lid. Bibs. Extra clothes. A Shout pen. A few gifts you set aside from birthdays or Christmas just to keep in this tub. Toys that have their noise-producing component broken (I leave "how" to your conscience). Worse case scenario: DVD and/or portable game system.

Although emergency kits don't stop the inevitable, they can make the some of the things we have to go through less painful. Except for teaching your kids to drive…you're on your own with that one.

Julius: The Baby of the World

By Kevin Henkes

"Julius is the baby of the world," chimed Lilly's parents.
"Disgusting," said Lilly.

Lilly used to be the best big sister in the world. Before she had siblings, that is.

After baby Julius is born, all that good sister business comes to a screeching halt. See, her parents loved the beady-eyed baby so much that it made Lilly hate him. She hated sharing her room with him. She hated having to whisper when he was napping. She hated his very parent-stealing presence and tried magic, among other things, to make him disappear.

But Julius, as her parents reminded her, wasn't going anywhere. And though they loved on Lilly, too, she continued to hate her brother.

Hated him, that is, until her annoying cousin, Garland, began to complain about Julius. Irritated by Garland's disparaging remarks (which ironically sounded just like Lilly's), Lilly shoves the baby into Garland's hands.

"Kiss! Admire! Stroke!" she demands with sudden sisterly pride.

It turns out that Julius was the baby of the world.

Especially to Lilly.

I'm sure Lilly's parents didn't mean to make her feel terrible when Julius was born. Any only child who is suddenly trumped by an adorable, freshly hatched baby brother or sister would probably act as rotten as Lilly did, watching their beloved parents cooing and drooling over someone other than him/her. Who *is* this impostor, anyway, and why are the lips that used to kiss *me* now kissing *him?*

No parent I know would admit (out loud) to favoring one child over the other, but ask any mom or dad a bit about each of their children and you only have to watch their facial expressions for about three seconds to see who The Golden Boy, The Athlete, or The Black Sheep is.

It's a hard trap to avoid, especially when one child exits the womb sweet and the next one, with a vendetta. The first four pictures we have of Anna, taken in quick succession at her birth, show her mad, madder, maddest, and some degree of anger for which there is no word in the English language. While other babies in the maternity ward were obediently nuzzling at their mother's breast, I was pacing the halls of the hospital in my polka-dotted nightgown with my inconsolable infant. She screamed *constantly*. Four years later, when the post traumatic stress started to fade a little, Elenia arrived, a child so phlegmatic she slept through the night at four days of age and never made any noise louder than a dove's coo to signal she was hungry.

Believe you me, I know the temptation of favoritism.

It is so easy to sigh, to shrug the shoulders in resignation, to roll the eyes when asked how the one child is doing. And just as easy to fall into a conversation about the perfections of the other, extolling her many gifts and multiple sweetnesses.

This does not, however, sisterly love promote.

Kids, not being entirely stupid, pick up on favoritism like they pick up on the fact Mommy Is Tense or Daddy Had A Rough Day. Friends and family can also feed this fire, drooling over the new baby while the gangly, buck-toothed nine-year-old watches on from her perch on the stairs.

But nothing pits siblings against each other like being in competition for favorite. Comparing them to each other (a la "Why can't you just be easy to get along with like your sister?") never motivates change. In fact, you can pretty much bank on it backfiring big time. Just ask Jacob and Esau.

Chubby, scrawny, homely, pigeon-toed, talkative, shy, knock-kneed, fuzzy-headed, shaggy, pale, freckled, bad-breathed, awkward, wiggly, or louder than a B-1 bomber, our children all want and need to be loved exactly as they are. Even, and especially, if their siblings *aren't* these things. And, as Lilly's story shows us, it's especially important to reassure them of this when ushering a new baby into the fold.

But it's okay if that love looks different for each child. I remember asking my mom who, out of her five children she loved best. She said, "I love you because you were my first." I interpreted this as her politically correct way of saying "You, without contest, darling." It was only later that I realized she probably told my sister that she loved her because she was the second, and my brother because he was the third and so on and so forth. The point is, we do love our children differently. I love one daughter's fun-loving, uncritical spirit. I love another's passion and drive. And I cherish the third's love of the written word and the fact she never wipes off my kisses. Choosing a favorite would be like being forced to choose between three kinds of pie: One is made from farm fresh peaches, double-crusted and sprinkled with turbinado sugar. Another is thick gooey pecan smothered in French vanilla ice cream. The third is a real whipped cream-covered lemon one. I love all three pies, but each for different reasons. Although it's taken years and much figurative head-banging, I'm slowly learning not to silently wish that this one was as self-controlled as the other, nor that this one was as industrious as her sister.

Oh, I forgot to tell you, your husband was talking to my husband the other night and he was wondering why it is that your sister lost all her baby weight in a month and you are still lugging around the chub from 1999. He also wondered why your hair color doesn't look as natural as your neighbor's does and why your enchiladas don't taste as good as the ones the pastor's wife makes.

See what I mean? Comparison stinks and never motivates change. Not the good kind, anyway.

I'm just joshing you about what your husband said. Actually, he told Ian he loves your curves and how your (natural or not) blond hair shimmers in the summer sun and how no one in the world whips up guacamole like you do.

You want to go make the man some brownies, don't you? 'Cuz nothing makes us love someone more than when they accept us exactly as we are, without comparing us to anyone else.

Just ask your kids.

TOOTLE

BY GERTRUDE CRAMPTON

"Red flags," muttered Tootle. "This meadow is full of red flags. How can I have any fun? Whenever I start, I have to stop. Why did I think this meadow was such a fine place? Why don't I ever see a green flag?"

Tootle was an engine-in-training in the Lower Trainswitch school where newbie engines took classes in Whistle Blowing, Stopping for a Red Flag Waving, and Pulling the Diner Without Spilling the Soup. The most important lesson, however, was Staying on the Rails No Matter What. No matter what else he did right, if Tootle didn't learn to Stay on the Tracks No Matter What, he would not graduate and become a Flyer between New York and Chicago.

This was hard, because Tootle loved to go fast. Stopping for a Red Flag Waving was hard enough for frisky young engines like him. But Staying on the Tracks No Matter What was sheer torture. So, sometimes, he did a Terrible Thing: He jumped the tracks to play in the meadow and chase horses and hold buttercups under his chin to see if he liked butter.

One day, Bill, the old engineer in charge of the school, noticed flower petals in Tootle's grill, and figured out what he was up to. He had to come up with a plan.

Bill placed townspeople all over the meadow with red flags and waited for Tootle to jump the tracks. Sure enough, he did. But everywhere he went, the people waved red flags. Again and again, Tootle had to stop, until he grew very frustrated. Finally, he saw it, a green flag waving wildly. There was Bill right on the track, a green flag in his hand. "This is the place for me," said Tootle. "There is nothing but red flags for locomotives that get off their tracks." From that day on, he Stayed on the Rails No Matter What and became a famous Flyer.

xcept for the fact Cooper is the caboose of our family instead of its engine, he and Tootle have a lot in common. Both are go-getters with lots of energy. They both are the kind of "people" who chafe under rules like Stopping for a Red Flag Waving and Staying on the Rails No Matter What. They want to run over here and dig a bunker in the back yard or run over there and make a slide from their room to the trampoline out back. They have a hundred ideas per minute and the energy of a Kansas tornado.

Kids like Cooper and Tootle wear parents (and teachers like Bill) out. So, every time they get off track, we start waving red flags at them. We tell them to keep their voices down and to fill in the giant hole fort in the back yard because the neighbors might think we're crazy, and that making a slide from their rooms to the trampoline is impossible. For every idea they come up with we come up a red flag to counter it. Pretty soon, they are as frustrated as Tootle was, not knowing what to do with their energy, their ideas, their creative genius.

I'm convinced that much of children's bad behavior comes because we wave far more red flags than green ones. We're quick to jump in with "Don't touch" and "Don't dig" and "Don't be loud," but we forget to substitute these red flags with the green flags of "Want to hold this neat shell (instead of that delicate crystal vase my great-grandmother brought with her when she immigrated from Ireland)?" or "Why don't you dig out by the tree instead of by mommy's heirloom rose bush?" or "Shut the door if you're going to be louder than a muffler-less motorcycle." It's easier to turn on the television or plug Jonny into the XBox or holler at him to be quiet than to help him brainstorm for creative alternatives.

I don't particularly like having a huge hole dug in my tiny backyard, but I allow Cooper to do it because I would rather he do something constructive than mope around and cause trouble simply because he is bored. My own parents channeled my own dervish intensity into playing the violin. Although that may have proved a mixed blessing (it took me two years to learn "Twinkle, Twinkle, Little Star"), it was also my savior, providing me with a productive outlet and keeping me from who-knows-what fate should I have had nowhere else to expend my energy.

If we're as wise as Bill was and wave as many green flags as our home owner's association will allow, maybe our children will eventually line up like Tootle did, to become great Two-Miles-A-Minute Flyers who Stay on the Rails No Matter What.

Curious George

By Margret and H.A. Rey

"George promised to be good. But it is easy for little monkeys to forget."

Poor George. Captured in Africa, he is forced to leave behind the only home he's ever known. He barely survives the journey to America and has to move in with a man who, for some never-explained reason, always wears a yellow hat. George is curious about his new home, as any monkey coming from the jungle to the big city would be. He can't help it! His new home is so mysterious, so full of unexplored corners and busy streets and telephone wires.

The trouble starts when the man in the yellow hat tells George to stay put and then leaves the house. But the fun-loving and mischievous George is far too curious to do that. Unsupervised, he gets himself into scrapes from which only the man with the yellow hat can rescue him.

As a mom, I look at the man in the yellow hat and think, okay, you're going to show a monkey how to dial the phone and smoke a cigar, then leave him alone in the house all day, and act surprised when he gets into a jam? Seriously??

But, as ridiculous as it sounds, sometimes parents of human babies do the same thing. We give our child a long leash and then, when he stretches it as far as he can go (or beyond), we shrug our shoulders and wonder what went wrong.

Jonny's parents, for example, like the man in the yellow hat, allowed him a wide berth. They didn't want to stifle his creative spirit. As long as he wasn't knocking down the pyramid of spaghetti sauce jars at the grocery store, he was a-okay. If he wasn't inflicting irreversible damage to the produce section, they were loving on the little guy. If he only said the s-word but not the f-word, they were cool. They gave him a play room with hundreds of toys and no rules. Want to jump on the guest bed in the corner? Jump away. Want to draw on the walls with chalk? Get scribbling. They would hate to stifle the little critter!

Susie's parents, on the other hand, gave her a short leash. When she was a baby, she played in a playpen with only one or two toys at a time. Her mother's friends wondered how she didn't get bored, but she never was. When she was older, her parents allowed her to play near them, but not to run off to the playground without asking. She had fun digging in the mud at their feet and never realized what she was missing out on around the corner.

As ironic as it sounds, Susie grew up feeling secure within her tight boundaries, while Jonny fought against the constraints of his looser ones. She was content. He kicked at the goads. She obeyed. Each day was a struggle for him. He never knew his boundaries because they were so far away he couldn't feel them. Susie's were near and clear, so she felt safe enough to have fun, satisfied with the few choices she had available to her. Studies consistently show that too many choices make kids both stressed and depressed, meaning Jonny's parents' attempts to be democratic hurt him, no matter how enlightened *they* felt giving him loose (or no) boundaries.

As "cute" as Curious George makes it look, the naughtiness that results from not enforcing boundaries is anything but. There's a fine line between allowing our monkeys to explore and allowing them to stomp on people's toes. If the man in the yellow hat had learned that sooner, H.A. Rey wouldn't have been able to produce so many fun sequels to his beloved book. As readers, we're grateful. But as parents, we should consider ourselves forewarned: Lucrative as presenting George as "curious" instead of downright naughty was for H.A. Rey, in real life, naughtiness profits nobody.

In real life, naughtiness is obnoxious. People don't like naughty children. Friends don't want to babysit naughty kids. Grandparents avoid spending time with naughty grandkids. Parents themselves don't enjoy naughty kids. Good kids don't enjoy naughty kids. I don't think even naughty kids enjoy themselves.

We need to do both our kids and ourselves a favor. We need to do their friends and future spouses a favor. Learn from the man in the yellow hat: Keep their leash short until they have enough self-control to manage a longer one. And remember: It's much easier to lengthen a short leash than it is to shorten a long one.

Because, no matter how cute the precocious primate is on the page, in real life, nobody likes a hooligan.

Don't Die on Molehills

lthough the man in the yellow hat could have managed George a bit better, some of Curious George's rascally behavior can be blamed on simple childish behavior. He wasn't being maliciously naughty, he just wasn't controlled very well. It brings up the question of mountains and molehills. As mamas, how are we to know the difference between mountains (naughty rebellion) and molehills (childish curiosity)?

Mountains are easy to spot, but, because they can be so irritating, molehills are often what we choose to die on. Here is a list of Curious George–type molehills which mamas can cross off their list of things to get excited about:

Spilling milk or any other liquid

Having untied shoes

Moving too slowly

Talking too quickly or with his mouth full of chicken nuggets

Going outside with wet hair

Wearing clothes that don't match

Needing (a reasonable number of) reminders to clean his/her room

Not getting ready fast enough

Not finishing his food once in awhile

Putting the fork on the right side of the plate, the knife on the right, and the spoon on top when it's his table setting day

Sending him to find something, only to find him an hour later reading the *Reader's Digest* in the bathroom

Smelling like a puppy

Having pants on backwards

Hair that sticks up on top

Slurping

Losing homework

Missing the edges of the yard during his first year of mowing

An obsession with counting and recounting his money

Handwriting that looks like a monkey's

Sticky kisses

Swinging his feet under the pew during church, especially if the sermon is boring

If there's one thing that keeps the hearts of parents and children knit together, it is having a Curious George mindset toward behavior. When we don't, and equate major no-no's (sassing parents, defiance, disobedience) with social or childish guffaws (forgetting to say thank-you, interrupting, not being able to zip their jacket), we risk hardening their hearts toward all discipline. Note, though, that the man with the yellow hat had a truly affectionate relationship with George. That is what we will have with our little monkeys, too, if we remember to differentiate between Curious George childishness and downright naughtiness.

Mary, Mary, Quite Contrary

MOTHER GOOSE

Mary, Mary, quite contrary,
How does your garden grow?
With silver bells, and cockle shells,
And pretty maids all in a row.

ccording to my thesaurus, being "contrary" means being antagonistic, opposite, or inconsistent. So it's not too much of a leap to assume that saying Mary was contrary was saying she most likely was a trial to her poor mother, perhaps the type of child who sits when told to stand and stands when told to sit.

I often feel like Mary and her mother reside inside my psyche, one saying one thing and the other saying the exact opposite in a complicated tug-of-war:

For example, I say that I value fitness, and insist that the only time I can possibly fit exercise into my busy, busy, really busy life is in the early morning, but I consistently refuse to go to bed early or set my alarm. Therefore, whole days and weeks go by without me twitching so much as a facial muscle.

I say I want sweet children, but I'm too tired to kick them (or myself) off the TV and properly discipline them.

I say I value a quiet, peaceful life, but I create a schedule that would kick Steven Covey's organized hind end.

I say I value quiet time with my family, but I invite friends over every other night.

I say I value a warm, loving bedtime for my children, but I push myself so hard during the day that I am toast by 7:30. Bedtime, therefore, is neither warm nor loving.

I say I value healthy eating, but buy Hostess cherry pies. In bulk.

I say I value creativity, but never actually pull out my paints.

I say I value my music, but my violin strings are shot and my bow in desperate need of a re-hairing. None of which I fix, even though a great violin shop is just down the road.

The contradiction between what we *claim to value* and what our lives *prove we value* causes an internal "Mary" crisis. It forces (or should force) a decision, telling us to "paint or get off the ladder." If we don't want to live a life of contrariness, like Mary lived, we need to decide if we are going to live according to what we value or if we are going to continue kidding ourselves. As a friend of mine once said, we complain because complaining is the most effort we can expend *without actually changing a darned thing*. In other words, it's easier to live in crisis mode than to do the hard work of orchestrating a life around those values that mean the most to us. It is easier to complain that I have no time to play my violin or that my clarinet reed has dried out or that I just don't have the time to read or that I am too rusty to get back into shape than to Just Do It. Mary was good at living with a foot in two worlds, but we shouldn't be.

Either we paint.

Or we get off the ladder.

But whining ad infinitum about what we wish we could do without any intention of taking even the tiniest baby step toward it, is neither healthy nor productive. The only good thing that might come of it is that we get a nursery rhyme written about us. And I bet Mary herself would tell us that kind of fame is way overrated.

Where The Wild Things Are

WRITTEN AND ILLUSTRATED BY MAURICE SENDAK

"…they roared their terrible roars and gnashed their terrible teeth and rolled their terrible eyes and showed their terrible claws till Max said, 'Be still!'"

This story is about the night Max disobeys his mother and is sent to his room without any supper. Here, his imagination takes over. Before long, his room has grown into a jungle and he takes a boat to where the Wild Things are. At first the monsters try to scare him out of his wits, but, if Max feels afraid, he never shows it. Instead, he tames them with his magic trick of staring into their yellow eyes until the monsters are at his disposal, ready to do his bidding. Later, when Max decides to go home, the monsters beg him not to leave, even offering to eat him if only he will stay. But Max says, most emphatically, "No!" And he goes home where he finds his dinner in his room where "it was still hot."

In *Where the Wild Things Are*, Max goes to the place his worst monsters live and learns to face and tame them. Scary as it sounds, he might be onto something.

When I was little, I used to have a couple of "monsters" that lived in my closet. First, I had an imaginary friend named Mary. She was this nice girl in a red dress and we got along splendidly until the day I woke up and realized that having an imaginary friend who lived in my closet was pretty creepy.

When I got a little older, my sister and I discovered another friend who lived in my parents' closet. His name was Chucky (no relation) and he wore green tights and a beret and was also a fun person to hang around with until we realized he, like Mary, was weird and then we got scared of him, and stopped going into my parents' bedroom even when mom sent us there to put her clothes away.

Eventually I outgrew my imaginary friends, but other creatures took their place:

Guilt (of things I had done, for things I hadn't yet done, but might, of things I might do in the future, of things that might hurt my children like sleeping in past seven and not offering enough fruits and vegetables which might impair their health and/or happiness). Worry (what if I miscarry, what if my baby is deformed, what if I die during childbirth, what if the baby gets sick, what if I am a terrible mother, what if Ian, despite his initial promise, turns out to be a terrible father, what if my child is ugly (yes, I'm that petty), what if I am like my mother, what if I am like my father, what if we never get rich, what if I have to drive this old Suburban forever, what if my child's teeth don't come in, what if I don't like my child, what if my child doesn't like me, what if my child has life threatening allergies, what if my teenager rebels and what if they grow up into terrible people even after all this hard work). Fear (of everything, but specifically: all-family flu bugs, car wrecks, floods, swimming without my glasses, throwing up, bunions, root canals, needles, dentists, doctors, talking on the phone, meeting strangers, the improper preparation of poultry, unwashed apples, people who wash lettuce in the bottom of their kitchen sinks, airplane travel, unfamiliar restrooms, and premature female pattern baldness).

I don't recall giving these monsters permission to move in, but move in they did and here they were, crammed into the closet of my mind so I hardly had any room for my sweaters or skirts. I'm no psychologist, but common sense said I needed to do some ghost busting.

Life itself has been a healer. Since you are reading the words on this page, you know that I did not, in fact, expire in childbirth. I did miscarry once, but had lots of friends to help me through it. Sometimes I offer lots of fruits and vegetables and sometimes I offer doughnuts and chocolate milk and my kids seem pretty robust. We have a couple of deformities amongst us, but carry on regardless. My children may or may not be ugly, but, if so, no one has mentioned it to me. I only had to drive the Suburban for twelve years before it got upgraded. My children like me sometimes, other times not so much; I've learned that the child liking me thing is overrated. The family has had only had two all-family flu bugs so far and lived to tell about it. The root canal, while slightly less exhilarating than opening presents on Christmas morning, wasn't all that bad. After six kids, I could insert my own IV line, so needles don't really throw me anymore. I've learned to use separate cutting boards. And my hair cutter assures me that if I were going to go bald, it would have happened already.

So much of what we worry about, dread, fear, and obsess over never comes to pass. The monsters in our closets, just like Max's, when exposed to the light of day and faced head on, are like the terrifying image on your bedroom wall that turns out to be nothing more than the shadow of the black dress you threw over a chair last night because you were too tired to hang it up after the party. Most of the time, we're shaking in our shoes over something as innocuous and fabricated as Mary or Chucky.

Trust me, don't listen to them; those two always were a couple of troublemakers.

Point is: Max faced his monsters. He didn't skirt around uncomfortable issues or avoid certain parts of town. He didn't see a therapist (although that is one solution) or read a self-help book. He didn't beat himself up or hide under his bed. He took his fears by the throat and made them his slaves, instead of the other way around.

Which is why I am going to introduce you to a new phrase, one I want you to remember and recite to yourself every time you avoid going to Target during flu season.

And when thinking about all the horrible ways you could potentially die.

And every time you have to skip ahead in *Chitty Chitty Bang Bang* because you can't bear to look at the kidnapper: ***"What Would Max Do?"***

Harold and the Purple Crayon

By Crockett Johnson

"But luckily, he kept his wits and his purple crayon."

Harold, the precocious bald baby, has a magic crayon that gets him out of all kinds of sticky situations. Like the time he drew a dragon to guard his apple tree and the dragon turned out to be a bit too frightening. As Harold backs away from the dragon, his hand with the crayon in it shakes, creating an ocean. He falls in, but comes up thinking fast and crawls into the boat he drew for himself. Later, he goes to the top of a tall mountain and accidentally falls off the not-yet-drawn half of the mountain. Again, his purple crayon saves him, this time by producing a hot air balloon that rescues him from an untimely death.

When Harold has had enough of adventuring and decides to go home, he can't find his way. Again, his crayon comes to the rescue, drawing hundreds and hundreds of windows until Harold remembers that the window in his room, his window, *is always around the moon. He draws the moon, with a window around it and, yes, there is his room. He makes his bed and "draws" up his covers and only then, when he falls asleep, does his handy dandy purple crayon drop to the floor.*

I'd like to have a crayon like that, wouldn't you? A nice fat one, maybe cornflower blue or magenta pink, stuck in my pocket for those times when things don't go as planned. Which for moms is, let's be honest, Every. Single. Day.

Forgot to make cookies for the Boy Scout troop? The purple crayon would draw up a plateful of fresh, gooey hot ones. Blew up at the kids? The purple crayon could erase those words and pen in some nicer ones. Housebound by a two-week slog of wet weather? Purple crayon would bring out the sun.

I'd definitely use it to resculpt my thighs.

I mean how handy would it be to have a magic tool that helps us figure out what to do when our company is four hours late or when our well-laid plans are dashed by sickness or a sprained ankle or bed rest or surprising news or when the first McDonald's after the 'No services for the next 100 miles' sign finally appears and claims their fryer is "broken?" Way handy, that's what it'd be.

Because almost no day goes as planned. I think it's safe to say that life with children *never* goes as planned. Now that my oldest is about to leave home, I am just beginning to learn to hold my plans ever so lightly, like a baby sparrow in the palm of my open hand. As planned, tonight's dinner will be fried potatoes and onions, kielbasa sausage, and cole slaw. In reality, I may be home too late to cook, my potatoes may have grown soggy in the bottom of the pantry since I last checked on them, one of the boys may have already eaten half the sausages, and I may be clean out of mayo. Anything can happen, at any moment, and it often does.

But, just like Harold, mamas have the choice to see those obstacles as manned and armed road blocks or as mere detours, with one of those friendly waver people smiling and directing us around the obstacles.

Of course, a mama might, like Harold in *Harold's Circus*, end up with her head in the lion's mouth. No one said mothering was safe.

But no matter. With her purple crayon firmly in hand, she'll make the best of it, just like Harold always did, replotting as needed, drawing up alternate blueprints, researching new paths, rerouting around dead ends, bending her plans to fit reality at every turn.

Purple crayons help us build a pirate birthday party complete with newspaper hats and felt eye patches when it rains on our child's long-awaited Slip-N-Slide extravaganza. Purple crayons help us discover that, even though we are so sports illiterate that we couldn't follow a toddler's football game, Jonny was born to wear shoulder pads and hurt people. Purple crayons lead us to buy $200 pianos on Craig's List to give wings to a child's dreams, even though we ourselves can't play "Chopsticks." Purple crayons find alternatives when a child can't read well. Purple crayons reveal a child's innate artistic talent or his ability to see in 3D, even though you hoped he'd be an avid reader or a miniature historian. Purple crayons help us flex when dreams are smashed by genetics, accidents, or Providence.

In my eighteen years of mothering, I've found that the more tightly I hold on to my plans, my way, and my schedule, the more difficult it is to access my trusty purple crayon. Things go much better when I remember to be flexible like Harold, keeping one tucked in my pocket, at the ready and sharpened to a fine point.

Alexander and the Terrible, Horrible, No Good, Very Bad Day

By Judith Viorst

"I could tell it was going to be a terrible, horrible, no good, very bad day."

Alexander was having a bad day. Nothing was going his way. First he went to sleep with gum in his mouth and got it stuck in his hair. Then his cat wouldn't sleep in his bed with him. Then there was no treat in his cereal box.

Such was the beginning of Alexander's rotten day. He fantasizes about running away to Australia, where surely no boy has bad days. But at the end of his terrible, horrible, no good, very bad day, his mother tells him that some days are just like that…even in Australia.

bet those who live Down Under would concur. No matter which hemisphere you live in, some days just stink. Even mateys have the occasional restless or interrupted night. Some days their bones hurt and their heads ache and there are crocodiles on their front porches. Even Aussies probably wonder how they will ever get through until bedtime, seeing as it's 120 degrees in the shade and the kangaroos are too sweaty to hop. Sometimes everything that can go wrong will, and all before eight in the morning, which, if you're following this analogy, is somewhere between one and four p.m. the previous day in the States.

No matter where you go in the world or who you are, no matter if your house has wheels or vaulted ceilings, no matter if you have one perfect child or twelve terrible children, bad days happen.

Blame it on the moon, the time of month, the season, the tilt of the earth on its axis, the tide, the horoscope, the day of the week, or Murphy's Law. Some days are so bad that I have to laugh at the statistical wonder of having so much go so wrong so fast in so short a time. Walking down the stairs first thing in the morning and stepping in a gooey hairball the cat spit up. Getting everyone ready for a fun day of biking along the river only to discover that seven of eight bikes have flat tires and the eighth, a missing seat. Packing the entire family for a trip to see grandparents only to have them call and say don't come, they have the flu. Finding the toddler using my brand new kitchen towels to clean up the dozen eggs he cracked on the kitchen floor. Day forty of both house showings and morning sickness.

Those are the small things and, on bad days, they're enough to do us in. As are stubbing the same toe for a third time, forgetting to rinse the conditioner out of your hair, spilling red Tylenol all over your new area rug, running errands with a dead cell phone, worrisome tooth pain, running out of diapers on a cold, wet day, a garbage disposal that quits disposing, hard-boiled eggs that won't peel on the day you said you'd bring deviled eggs to the BBQ, pilled sheets, shedding dogs, days too hot for the kids to play outside, nasty phone calls, a too-long to-do list.

Just one of these isn't so bad, but start coupling them together and you have the ideal conditions for the Perfect Storm of a bad day.

Bad days are, er, bad, so I want them to be over with as quickly as possible just like Alexander did, don't you? If I feel sick, I want to feel better. Stat. Dope me up on Dayquil, give me my heating pad, and tuck me into soft sheets with a movie and a box of tissues. We'll knock this puppy out.

But, the longer I've been a mama, the more I see that Alexander's mom was onto something: Bad days happen. Period. And, to take it a step further, if bad days are inevitable, is it possible I can learn not to just grit my teeth and endure, but to learn something valuable from them?

There is a reason for bad days, although don't try to tell that to someone in the middle of one. Bad days slow us down. Bad days sober us and give us empathy for other people who are having their own bad days. Bad days give us a perspective that running from one spectacular 24-hour period to the next does not. Bad days force us to think and to reevaluate. Bad days can make us so dissatisfied with the status quo that we finally have the impetus to change. Bad days can energize us to start over, to bury the hatchet, to seek resolution, or to end a toxic relationship. Bad days can be indicators that something deeper is going on, something to which it would behoove us to pay attention. Bad days remind us to train our kids better, to be more proactive, to get organized, and to plan ahead. Bad days prompt us to look in the mirror and see if we are part of the problem.

Then again, there's always the off chance that it's just a plain old garden variety, standard-issue, terrible, horrible, no good, very bad day. In that case, don't worry about it.

They have those even in Australia.

The Taming of the Shrew: A Short Treatise on PMS

t's noon on Monday and the morning has been terrible. The baby has whined since breakfast and wouldn't take his nap. The three-year-old used too many pieces of paper for his drawing, and they're scattered all over the kitchen floor. The kindergartner refused to eat his oatmeal, which is now congealing in the refrigerator for another ~~battle~~ try at lunch.

And your head isn't exactly hurting, but it feels tight around your ears, like a facelift gone south, and every sound the kids make is ricocheting around your head like a rogue bullet. The husband promised to call and tell you if the babysitter can or cannot babysit tonight, but hasn't. When you called your mom to ask if she could do it, she gave you some cockamamy story about being "busy." You then bite your older son's head off when he calls at the last minute to ask for a ride home from his friend's house.

Just about the time you find yourself on your knees with your head in the back of the baking cabinet looking for the rest of the Christmas chocolate, you realize, no, you aren't going crazy.

You have PMS.

Which you will have, approximately four thousand times in the next thirty-odd years.

And, to add insult to injury, being a mama means that not only do you have the monthly hormones that are common to all women, but the extra installment that comes with pregnancy, childbirth, and nursing. Each. And. Every. Time.

Hormones happen. And—brace yourself—they will happen to your girls, too. I have a friend who says you haven't really lived until you have a house full of girls on the same cycle.

So, what's a mama to do? I certainly haven't mastered the art of PMS management (ask my kids), but I have friends who've taught me a few clever ways to tame the shrew in me whenever the hormones strike.

First, mark it down. I now write my dates on my bathroom mirror with eyeliner so I'm reminded to incorporate Operation Shrew Taming. No matter how much I think I will remember when it's due, I don't. Writing it on a calendar is another option, but half the time I can't find my calendar. I'm vain, so no matter what, I always look in the mirror. So, for me, the mirror works. Just don't forget, you get fussy a few days *before* that date.

Second, some of my friends mark it in their husband's Day Timer. This only works if, one, you have a husband, and, two, he uses a Day Timer. It's not his job to tip toe around you when you're moody, but a Nice Husband might anyway. And rub your shoulders in lieu of defending himself when you lay into him for coming home five minutes late. And maybe even bring home some coffee ice cream without being asked. Whatever he does, let's pray he doesn't commit the Unpardonable Sin and ask, "Do you have PMS?"

Which, of course, you *don't*.

Last, the best defense is a good offense.

Operation Shrew Taming means clearing your schedule as much as possible on wobbly days. This isn't the time to book back-to-back appointments with prickly clients.

Operation Shrew Taming means stocking up on frozen pizza and delegating dinner detail.

As far as it is in your power, OST is the time to avoid stressful interactions. Don't call your professor for feedback on your thesis idea or ask your neighbor if they would please get a less barky dog.

Don't plan huge projects on these days. This is not the time to purge the basement or paint the garage floor.

Be kinder to yourself. Don't feel guilty for caving up a bit, taking long baths, or reading a book that has absolutely zero educational value.

Ramp up your exercise and make sure you are being religious with your daily vitamin. On the other hand, don't beat yourself up if you accidentally polish off the Oreos.

Whatever you do, if you are feeling wenchy, learn from me, dear reader, and keep yourself off Facebook. If you have to spew, do it in a journal. Or into a pillow. Or to the dog.

Taming our inner shrew once a month isn't easy. But it's good practice, because you know what's next?

Menopause.

Frog and Toad are Friends

By Arnold Lobel

"Dear Toad, I am glad that you are my best friend. Your best friend, Frog."

Frog and Toad were about as different as two amphibians can be. Frog was green and slimy. Toad was brown and rough. Frog was eternally cheerful and optimistic. Toad was grouchy and negative. But, despite their differences, Frog and Toad stuck together. Through dark winter days and lost coat buttons, through sick days and days with no mail, through bad swim suits and people laughing at them.

Because that's the way best friends are.

hen the book *The Divine Secrets of the Ya Ya Sisterhood* came out I didn't buy it because I didn't like the look of its cover. I'm petty and small that way.

Eventually, however, I not only bought it, but read it. That book resounded so profoundly in my psyche that I had to call my sisters and have them read it, too. Why it had such an impact, I'm not sure. After all, the main character and I were about as far apart as two people can be:

Sidda Lee was single and had a very understanding boyfriend.

I have been married for two decades to a man who used to be understanding before I wore him out.

Sidda Lee had a mom who was an alcoholic Catholic from Louisiana Cajun country.

My mom is a teetotaling Southern Baptist from Electra, Texas, which, for those who are interested, is halfway between Punkin Center and Bugscuffle.

So I'm not sure why that book grabbed me by the neck, slammed me to the ground, and hogtied my heart.

Maybe it was the universal dynamic between mother and daughter that did it. My mom and I certainly tussle from time to time, so that's a possibility. And that book talked a lot about cold Cokes being drunk on the front porch and I love cold Cokes, especially those drunk on the front porch.

What really pulled me in, I think, was the dynamic between the four best friends, the self-proclaimed "Ya-Yas." The book follows the trajectory of these four women's lives as they go through all sorts of trials, from bad husbands to alcoholism to the terrifying act of raising children. They're more sisters than friends, occasionally squabbling, always brutally honest, but, like Frog and Toad, sticking together no matter what.

Wouldn't it be nice to have your own set of Ya-Yas? Close friends who go through the ups and downs of life together, who tell each other the truth, who accept each other no matter what?

I love my Ya-Yas dearly, despite the fact some of us are as different from each other as Frog and Toad were. Friendship is that way sometimes. One of my Ya-Yas is a quiet vegetarian who loves animals almost more than she loves people. I love steak. One is single, travels the world, and runs. I have been married twenty-two years, have never set so much as a toenail in Tijuana despite having lived in Southern California for five years, and only run when I hear a child say, "I think I'm gonna throw up." One always sees the glass half-full, while I fight seeing it not only bone dry, but cracked down one side. One hates to use bleach, while I'd drink the stuff if I thought it would render me germ free.

But friends we are, and, like Frog and Toad, we complement each other. I need their sugar and they need my salt (or so they say). I need their hopefulness and they need my grounding. Somehow, we work and are both the better for it.

These days, we're a scattered bunch: One of my Ya-Yas lives in Oregon. We met on the first day of kindergarten and held hands at recess until we were about twelve. I met one Ya-Ya when our husbands went off to war together and I had to be a daddy to her new baby. One Ya-Ya and I talk about writing and mothering and keep each other off cliffs. I have Ya-Yas in my city and Ya-Yas who travel the globe. Here a Ya, there a Ya, everywhere a Ya-Ya.

I wish they all lived closer, but most days it's enough to know they are—like Fievel's sister in *An American Tail*—Somewhere Out There. I know I can show up at three in the morning and they will open the door and make me a sandwich, no questions asked, even if I'm in my jammies with no makeup on. That's saying something, folks.

In medieval times, master architects, masons, and craftsmen built beautiful cathedrals whose spires seemed to pierce the heavens. But, because of their size, those walls were unstable. The builders had to add buttresses, long arms that reached from the ground to the side of the walls, to keep them from collapsing. Originally after-market add-ons, buttresses are now inseparable from the majestic beauty of the cathedral.

Ya-Yas are our buttresses. They hold us up when we are weak. They support us when life is unstable. They offer grounding when our worlds are upside down. And, eventually, like cathedrals and buttresses, we too can become inseparable, our lives woven so tightly together you can hardly tell where one stops and the other starts.

We all need a Toad to our Frog or a Frog to our Toad. In other words, we all need Ya-Yas. Mamas especially need Ya-Yas. We've got to have those safe people we can be 100% ourselves with, backdoor friends who see us first thing in the morning and still agree to look at us. We need people we can depend on to comfort us when the thumbscrews of life start to tighten.

However you do it, find yourself some Ya-Yas and dig in deep with them. Do life together. Pick them up when they fall and allow yourself to be picked up when you fall.

Whatever you do, don't wait until you need one to find one, for you never know when you'll need your Ya-Yas.

The Magic Fish

Adapted by Freya Littledale

"No," said the fish. "She wants too much. She cannot be queen of the sun. She cannot be queen of the moon and the stars. Now she must go back to the old hut."

The fisherman's wife in this story isn't satisfied with her little hut by the sea. So when her husband encounters a magic fish, she starts in with a list of demands: First she wants a pretty house, then she wants a castle, then she wants to be queen of the land, and, finally, she demands to be queen of the sun and the moon and the stars.

The fish, although irritated, is patient and indulging up to the last request. But, when she asks to be queen of the sun and the moon and the stars, he takes it all back and puts her back in her hut, where she remains to this very day.

ave you ever heard the term "fishwife"?

It's not a flattering one.

A fishwife is a woman who is contentious, troublesome, and cranky. Apparently, all that net mending and fish cleaning took its toll. Demanding, selfish, and pushy, the wife in *The Magic Fish* personifies "fishwife" perfectly.

What a wench. I mean, I would never be that way, would you? Buy one thing, grow dissatisfied with it after a few weeks. Buy something else. Grow bored with it, too. Move on to something else which doesn't satisfy either.

Who, me be discontent like that fishwife? Never.

No, I've never been dissatisfied with my clothes, the homes I've lived in, my kids, my husband, my friendships, my body, my station in or my season of life. Not once, no siree, not me.

Oh, wait, there was this *one time…*

We lived in a huge, rambling house on a cultivated acre on the edge of town. My husband had a good job and we were initially thrilled with the house.

But, just moments after moving in, that house started to make me miserable. I hated the old faded gray carpet and couldn't wait to put in wood floors. We put in glossy hardwood floors, but they made my knees and hips hurt and every tiny sound ricochet throughout the house like a sonic boom. Moving furniture without scratching the floors was like trying to play hockey without disturbing the ice. I spent hours each week dust mopping and scrubbing that gorgeous floor, and fretting over each new mark or divot that appeared.

The many windows with their beautiful wood casings also grieved me. The wood grew dry in the summer from the sun and in the winter from the cold. It cracked in places. The screw-out panes sometimes refused to screw back in and we'd have to go outside and push them back into place when it started to rain or the mosquitos got bad. I began to price shop for new windows, only to realize replacing them was hopelessly out of budget.

We bought new leather couches for the living room because every cute house I'd ever seen in magazines had leather couches. But ours were always so stiff and freezing cold that we never sat on them. The huge vaulted ceilings made the house feel cold and impersonal. The kitchen cabinets were dated and worn. We would have loved to have the use of the cavernous basement, if only we could get it finished. The yard was so big I could only afford to landscape one thumb-sized flower bed. The mowing and weeding of the yard and the constant cleaning of the house filled every weekend hour.

Being forced to downsize rescued me from the season of my discontent. With our small rental home I have no expectations, so every halfway decent feature is a bonus. It's easy to clean and easy to mow. My knees are recovering. And weekends are free for things like fun.

Do you ever get dissatisfied, like the Fisherman's Wife and me? Not happy until all home improvement projects are done? Owning a wardrobe that is never big or updated enough? Longing for the rewarding job you had before children? Wanting to move closer to family or away from the rain or next to the ocean?

None of these things is bad in and of itself, but a cycle of discontent is. It poisons today in hopes for tomorrow. Like the Fisherman's Wife learned the hard way, discontent is a cruel taskmaster. Because living only for that wonderful day in the nebulous future when your house/career/life/body are just exactly the way you want, isn't living at all.

Adults aren't the only ones who get stuck in cycles of discontent. Kids do, too. And it's our job to help them identify what is happening. In our house, we call this syndrome 'birthday-itis' because it strikes in full force two weeks to the minute before any child's birthday. There is something about knowing their special day is coming that births unreasonable and never-ending demands. The relentless gift and cake requests. Asking to add one more friend to the invitation list. Begging to open just one teensy weensy present ahead of time or to move the party date up (Cooper once went this route, philosophizing that it would be in my benefit to just 'get it over with'). Frankly, they are unfit to live with until the holiday we recently invented called The Blessed Day After Their Birthday.

What's great about birthday-itis is that, once a year, it gives me the perfect chance to point out to each child how insatiable discontent is. Left unfettered, there is no end to the list of wishes of new toys to buy and places to go and experiences to have. Bucket and Christmas lists are great, as long as you can live happily in the meantime. Wanting a Lego set is fine, as long as you don't get lured into thinking 'just one more' is going to make you happy, as long as that one set doesn't lead to a constant browsing of Amazon's Lego page, lusting after one more Turbo Tank, one more Clone, one more Drop Ship…

(Cooper, you listening?)

What the Fisherman's Wife didn't realize is that more is just that…more. More to clean. More to store. More to pick up. More to keep track of. More to manage. More to lose, as she sadly found out.

More is an unending path with no satisfying destination. More only leads to more. And, sometimes, that "more" is just more trouble. And who—besides the Fisherman's Wife, apparently—wants that?

Those Darned Joneses

ou know them. Perhaps they live next to you or share your pew at church. The Joneses are the ones with the perennially fresh-scrubbed children with apple-pink cheeks, the ones who never take a naughty child out to spank. They own a cute little Craftsman-style home in that one darling neighborhood where every house has a huge front porch and a porch swing. They have a bumper sticker on their Land Cruiser that says, "Debt-free and loving it!" She is a size two on her bloated days and he has the carefree look of the financially secure. Their naturally curly-haired children sleep from seven in the p.m. to seven in the a.m., giving them time to work out as a couple and have a healthy breakfast together each morning before work. Pottery Barn furniture fills their home, a plate of homemade muffins often adorns their reclaimed barn wood dining room table. Their biggest problem is deciding which Caribbean island to visit *this* year and who should get the joy of babysitting their three darling and perfectly behaved offspring.

And—admit it—you are jealous. Green from head to toe

over their apparently effortless success, their heirloom rose bushes that blossom twice as often as yours do with only a fraction of the finger-pricking effort, their refrigerator, stocked with organic produce, that never smells of onion or tunafish like yours does.

You'd never say so aloud, but it's true: You privately criticize the Joneses. Their children are good because all three of them are Type-B relaxed types, you say, not exciting like your Type-A's. They have no car payment because their parents lavish cash gifts upon them every Christmas and birthday, you say. Their marriage is happy because one of them must be caving, you justify.

You rank your own children, lifestyle, and marriage against theirs and yet, no matter what shortcomings you dream up, they still come out ahead. And you can't stand it. Why doesn't she have to work and you do? Why hasn't he started to bald when your husband is already doing the comb-over? Why are their kids so sickly sweet while yours bicker all the live long day?

Dear mamas, *we aren't the Joneses.* And the truth is, we don't know how they paid off their cars or if their cars are paid off at all. For all we know, their children may act good in church, but be sullen and uncooperative at home. And we don't know how hard she sweats or how hungry she gets to keep that size two frame.

Comparing ourselves to another family or to another mama is as productive as painting a skyscraper with a toothpick. I know because I've done it (the comparing part, I mean). I've wished I was soft-spoken like the pastor's wife or articulate like my daughter's English teacher. I've envied other people's Restoration Hardware houses and been ashamed of my own cookie-cutter special. I've looked at other children and wondered how I failed to provide mine with braces, music lessons, a good example.

Where does such comparison get me, though? Squeezing a Clydesdale into a butterfly mold just makes a mess. We'd be better off to accept that we aren't the Joneses and move on.

Let them have what they have. Let them be who they are. And channel your energy not into envying them, but into being the best you you can be. Maybe you'll find out you don't like growing roses anyway. Maybe tulips are your thing. Maybe you actually prefer your husband to look more like Yul Brynner than Grizzly Adams. Maybe your children act up more because they are full of ideas, curiosity, and an insatiable zest for life. Maybe your house is messy because your family is busy making art together. Maybe you eat dinner late because your husband has a new booming business. Maybe your cars are rusty because you travel all the time. Maybe your house is dusty because you'd rather spend time playing board games than cleaning.

Whatever the case, embrace it. Revel in it. Be the family you were meant to be. Who knows? Maybe the Joneses are jealous of *you*.

If You Give a Mouse a Cookie

By Laura Joffe Numeroff

"And, chances are, if he asks for a glass of milk, he's going to want a cookie to go with it."

The mouse in this story is given a cookie, but then wants some milk to go with it. But he's not content with that. He then asks for a straw to go with the milk. Then a napkin to wipe his face. Then a haircut for the whiskers he noticed when wiping his face. Then a broom to clean up the whiskers he just cut off. Then a box to nap in because he's tuckered out. Then he wants a story. Then paper and crayons. Then a pen. Then scotch tape. Then more milk. Then—you guessed it—another cookie. Because we all know that cookies, to be properly enjoyed, need milk to go with them.

If ever there is a book that more perfectly illustrates the power of whining, I don't know what it is. Laura Numeroff captures the childish trait so perfectly I suspect she has a few mice of her own at home who regularly beat her down with their never-ending demands, just like the mouse who stars in this book.

The idea that whining is just part of being a kid has become so widely accepted that one wonders if it is written down in a parenting bible somewhere. But, as we learn in *If You Give a Mouse a Cookie*, children aren't to blame for whining. Parents are.

What? Blasphemy, they cry. But yes, it's true. Just like the mouse owner in this book was to blame for the mouse's theatrics that exhausting afternoon with the cookie, we parents are to blame for whining.

See, our children whine not because they are children, but because somewhere along the way whining worked. One day—we probably can't even remember when—they pressured us for something. We gave in, and the memory of that got branded into their psyches along with other things we inadvertently taught them like, If I Scream I Get An Ice Cream Cone and Make Me Wear Those Pants And I Will Make Your Life a Living Hell.

To wit, take the case of Susie who asks you if she and her BFF, CiCi, may have a sleepover.

Now, tonight is a very bad night for a sleepover. You have plans with The Man for a date night. The house is a wreck, the plumber is stopping by in the morning to fix the toilet, and there is no fun food in the house. Plus, you are tired.

Of living.

So you say, most emphatically, *No*. And you really mean it. You are, in fact, an impenetrable fortress of *No*.

Oh, please, mom, they say. We haven't had a sleepover in two months and CiCi is leaving for the Bahamas with her family on Monday, they say. It will be two more weeks until we can even *begin* to think about another sleepover, they say.

And now commences The Dance—the tippee toe shuffle—and, if the other girl is present, she too is hopping up and down, both of them with hands pressed together as if in prayer.

Please, please, please!!! Oh, Mom, pleeeeease! Oh, Mom, Mom, Mom!

You pause. You sigh. You really, *really* don't want a sleepover.

You wanted a date night, you say.

You're so tired your hair hurts, you whimper.

The girls, instead of pitying your obvious internal struggle, up the ante, acting weepy and just so darned sad. You look at their tearful faces and suddenly remember how it was to be ten-years-old and willing to shave five years off your life if it meant having a sleepover. The fingernail painting. The Ho-Hos. The wonderful gritty I-have-only-slept-five-minutes feeling the next day.

You start to waffle. You can, after all, go on a date another night. You can get by with only one toilet for another 24 hours. You can run to the store later. You can sleep when you're dead.

So you agree. *BUT JUST THIS ONCE*, you say in one last attempt to retain some semblance of authority.

And, in that moment, Mama, you have given your daughter enough ammunition to float her comfortably through her teen years. You have just taught her that if she is only persistent, charming, and pitiful enough, you will give in. And, being a smart girl, she will remember this moment more clearly than she remembers how to spell her own name.

The mouse in this story would have hated to live at my house because my rule is this: You get nothing you beg for. Ever.

If we are in the store and you insist on Juicy Fruit and start The Dance, you get nothing.

If you want a Coke and begin to squeal, you go thirsty. Always. And, if you need a reminder, I am more than happy to give you one.

This is as effective as that psychological test where they put a glass wall between some pirañas and some goldfish. No matter how hard they try, the pirañas cannot reach those fish. After butting their heads against the wall for a certain million number of times, the pirañas give up to the point where, even when the glass is removed, they don't try to eat the goldfish.

It's called extinguishing behavior. And it works with kids as well as fish.

Horton Hatches the Egg

By Dr. Seuss

"I meant what I said and I said what I meant...An elephant's faithful one hundred percent!"

Poor Horton, conned into egg-sitting by Lazy Mayzie the bird, didn't realize it was going to be an all-season job. But he promised her he wouldn't leave her egg and he meant it. Through snow and through sleet, with icicles on his feet, he sat and he sat and he sat on that egg...

nlike Horton, sometimes we mamas say things we don't mean. We say, Jonny take off your shoes at the door and yet here comes Jonny running right through our freshly mopped kitchen floor with his muddy tennis shoes still on and we do nothing but sigh and grab the mop. And we say Stop banging that stick on the piano, but the banger keeps banging and we do nothing about it. And we say, emphatically, No! you may *not* go out and play on the

trampoline because it's raining and the trampoline might be slippery and you might fall and get a concussion and yet we find just a few moments later several young people jumping away, happily soaked to the bone, as slippery as eels.

Sometimes we mindlessly issue orders like these. And so we reinforce them (meaning we don't) just as mindlessly. So many words are coming out of our mouths that we can't possibly keep track of, much less follow through with, what we said/threatened/promised.

But, for some strange reason, we're shocked when our kids ignore us on the rare occasion we actually *do* mean what we say. Stay out of the street, for example. That's not a directive you can bank on repeating too many times. Children need to obey the first time or risk learning the hard way, should they survive the experience. But because we said Don't run through the house with your shoes on and we said Quit banging the piano with that stick and we said No you cannot jump on the trampoline while it is raining and we didn't mean any of those things, our children assume we don't mean *any* of what we say, including, Don't run into the street.

If heard at all, sometimes we speak in a way that does not send the signal that we mean business. Our words are taken as suggestions, advice someone may want to take someday in the future should ever the spirit move. Just not today and certainly not *right now*. Our words are not heeded because we, ourselves, don't expect them to be heeded. How many times have you shouted out an order, watched it directly ignored or disobeyed, and chuckled to yourself that "Kids will be kids?"

Yes, kids will be kids, but mothers must be mothers. If

we bark out meaningless commands followed by impotent threats concluding with nonexistent discipline, we shouldn't be surprised when our children don't listen to us.

But Horton knew better. He meant what he said and he said what he meant. And this was easier than it could have been because he kept what he said simple: Sit on the egg until it's lazy mother, Mayzie, returned. Did he have a three-page-long list of his tasks as egg-sitter? No. He had *one* policy and he determined to follow it no matter what. Likewise, if we issue copious off-the-cuff orders to our children, not even we can remember what we said. We cannot remember (must less follow up with) who didn't rinse his dishes or who forgot to take out the dog if those are two of thirty commands we mindlessly dished out. It would be better to issue one order that we intend to follow up on than thirty we don't. Be wise, mamas, in what you ask for, because saying what you mean and meaning what you say means…

…if you tell your eight-year-old son that if he leaves his bicycle on the porch one more time you will take it away for the summer, you better be prepared to take away the bike. For the entire summer.

…if you tell your daughter that if she is home even one minute after her curfew, she is grounded for a week, you better be willing to ground her for a week at 12:01a.m.

…if you tell your teenaged son that if he plays video games before finishing his homework you will ground him from Black Ops for a month, not finishing that English paper means you do just that.

…if you tell the kids to go to bed, don't ignore the fact they are still pajammy-less and watching their movie thirty minutes later.

Horton knew that come here means come here. Now means now. Stop means stop.

He might have been weight challenged and overqualified for his job as egg sitter, but you have to give him credit—no matter how tough things got, he meant what he said and said what he meant.

The question is, do we?

Good Dog, Carl

By Alexandra Day

"Look after the baby, Carl. I'll be back shortly."

When Mom puts Carl, the family's friendly Rottweiler, in charge of the baby while she goes out for the day, we question many things, one of which is her sanity. But Carl and baby have a marvelous time. They jump on the bed, put on mother's makeup, slide down the laundry chute, "swim" in the fish tank, dance in the living room, eat a snack, take a bath, clean up the house, and finally, fall asleep. When mother comes home and Carl is rewarded by a pat on the head and a "Good dog, Carl!" you can almost hear the subtext: "Thanks for not eating the baby, Carl."

arl, despite the bad rap of his particular breed, is one great Baby Whisperer. Notice the following: how many times he reminds the baby to get in bed, how many times he nags the baby to clean up after himself, how exasperated he becomes when baby doesn't go to sleep on schedule.

The answer is...*none.*

Part of it might be because Carl is a dog.

Part of it might be because he knows what some parents don't: That a glut of words goes in one baby ear and out the other. We human parents talk, direct, shush, remind, and otherwise fill our children's heads with so many words that they become deaf to them. Note the mother who must always talk louder and louder to be "heard." Do her children not "hear" her or are they just not listening?

Hm.

Repeated phrases and constant reminders are simply not taken seriously. A drone is tuned out. A continual dripping is ignored. Consider the following:

"Golly darn it kid I can't believe you did it again how many times do I have to tell you not to get on the counter and get into the sugar and spread it all over your hands and your face and look now, your feet are covered and it's all going to make a big goopy mess all over the counters I just cleaned five minutes ago and don't you know that every year kids just your age are falling off counters just like ours, especially ones that are sticky and slippery like this one and, look! What are you doing now? Licking your fingers? Sucking on your toes? Weren't you outside earlier? Don't you know what kind of diseases reside on your toes? Weren't you walking around where the dogs play? Oh my gosh, don't you know the kinds of germs, insects, WORMS that get on your feet and wherever your feet are, which is now on top of this counter and now on your fingers and NOW in your mouth! Which probably means you will be sick within a day and I will have to stoop over the toilet with you while you are, in fact, quite miserable. Don't you know what causes these things and haven't I told you at least one kajillion times to keep off the counter and wash your hands and don't get into the sugar and whatever you do, not to lick your fingers?"

Compare that to Carl's approach:

"Honey, get off the counter, go wash your hands, and keep out of the sugar."

Carl knew better. He directed with as few words as possible. In return, he was respected and obeyed.

Despite being the wrong gender and the wrong species, you have to admit, Carl made one darned good mama.

The Emperor's New Clothes

Hans Christian Anderson

The Emperor was a proud man who loved beautiful clothing. One day he hired two tailors who promised to sew him a gorgeous outfit made out of thread that, ironically, was invisible to anyone not fit for their position or who was "just hopelessly stupid."

Once the men got to work, neither the emperor nor any of his ministers could see the thread the tailors were supposedly weaving into cloth, but they didn't dare admit it lest anyone think them, like I said, unfit for their position or hopelessly stupid. Before long, the tailors dressed the emperor in his lovely new gown and, although he still could not see the clothing and felt he looked, in fact, quite naked, he marched with great pomp down the street, flaunting his new duds. No one told him he didn't have any clothes on because they, too, were afraid of looking stupid.

Finally, a young child, who didn't know what was going on, exclaimed, "But he isn't wearing anything at all!"

amas can play Emperor all too well, in that, sometimes we're so afraid of looking "hopelessly stupid" that we ignore the blind spots in our parenting rather than listen to obvious truth. Don't believe me? Try going within five miles of even hinting that your neighbor's child needs to play nicer and watch her snap her purse shut and go off in a huff.

What is it about mothering that makes us so sensitive? In any other situation in life, in marriage or at work or on sports teams, constructive criticism may not be fun to hear, but it's at least carefully considered. Feedback is how we learn to get a better backhand in tennis, how to quit splicing in golf, how to cut our swim times. It's how we learn to sew buttonholes, how to crochet without knots, and how to make a tender pot roast. It's how we learn to manage people well and learn how to communicate effectively. But the same woman who will patiently listen to a 360 review in the office will come unglued if her mother-in-law dares suggest she not die on the hill of making her child wear the blue pants instead of the green.

Now, of course, people are quick to offer unsolicited advice, so not every comment can or should be taken to heart. But neither should we stop up our ears if someone says something negative about our children or our mothering. Especially if that someone knows us well and isn't known for being mean-spirited. We should especially listen to what others say if we are repeatedly hearing the same thing. If three people have said that your son is biting their children, you need to accept, however difficult it might be, that your son may actually be biting children.

It's easy to look at the Emperor strutting naked down the street with nothing but his crown on and think, "What a fool! Why can't he just be honest with himself and admit he has no clothes on?" Or to observe the other people in the castle and wish that *someone* had the courage to tell the poor man the truth. But no one, except the boy at the end, did. Like the Emperor, it's not easy to look at ourselves or at our parenting and say, come on, people, lay the truth on me, I can take it!

A friend once told me that if I were more consistent in my discipline, Emily would obey me better. I resented this advice because it came from a woman who didn't yet have children. But she was right. I would have been a fool to ignore her comment, no matter how much it upset me at the time. Another time, a woman I knew said that she noticed we all seemed to pigeon hole Anna in a certain behavior. She, too, was right, and, after I stopped fuming, I began to notice exactly what she was talking about and we are learning to avoid doing that.

No one likes to be criticized. Especially mamas, because we're having to hold a line in the sand over so many issues already—schooling decisions, discipline methods, special diets, stances on immunizations, etc. By no means should we be wishy washy, tightening the reins when the grandparents visit and loosening them once they leave or expecting one kind of behavior in the store and another at home, just because we're afraid of what people might think. However we'd be as foolish as the Emperor was to ignore our blind spots. The Proverbs say, "Faithful are the wounds of a friend." It may hurt to have our best friend tell us our daughter was a selfish brat all afternoon (hopefully she'll phrase it gentler than that), but it might be the wake-up call we need to adjust our discipline with her. In the end, criticism can be a "faithful wound" if it becomes the catalyst for a change that is beneficial to both us and our children.

Hearing something negative about our children is one of the hardest things a parent has to hear. But, the next time you're tempted to get defensive over someone's criticism, picture the Emperor in his birthday suit walking along the streets with everyone gaping at his private parts just because neither he nor anyone else had the guts to face the truth.

Who knows, it might just save you from your own jaunt through the city, naked as a newborn.

The Story of Hester

A HOMEMADE STORY

y family grew up next door to a little boy I will call Hester. Now, Hester's mother just loved her little darling. In her eyes Hester could do no wrong. They spent their days walking along their "country road," at the edge of our Washington neighborhood, picking wildflowers that grew in the ditches and attaching bits of leaves to a piece of tape little Hester wore on his wrist for just such occasions. To the average observer, they made a darling pair, Hester with his wide basset-hound eyes and his eternally enthusiastic mother.

One day, I was called upon to babysit little Hester and, even though he was six years old, it was the first time he had been away from his mother, except for his circumcision, and it was a Big Deal. He ate special foods and had a rigorous routine that I was to follow, but the hardest thing of all was giving the proper amount of attention to the boy whose every minute accomplishment was met with wild clapping and "Yes! Yes! You're doing it, Hester! Great job!! Keep going!! Yes! Yes!"

I never understood this, because, in our home, attention was something you stood at, not something you gave a child just for being alive.

That afternoon, Hester stared at me expectantly as I looked around the kitchen which was, quite literally, wallpapered from floor to ceiling, with Hester's attempts at "art." Crayon scribblings of two lines crossing in the middle had a cursive comment to the side, "Hester, GREAT WORK! I can see that you were remembering our last visit to the museum as you drew this! Move over Picasso, here he comes!" Each paper had these sorts of comments written on them, even though, to me, they looked more like the time I watched the elephants at the zoo fling paint onto cardboard.

Shelves against one wall held dried play-dough "ash trays" that looked like something a cat would spit up, while the kitchen table held his piece de resistance, a paper mache "globe" of hardened glued on newspapers where his mother had written with juicy red marker, "Hester lives HERE" on top of a grocery store ad for Lego panty hose.

For your sake I'll skip the bulk of my endless afternoon with little Hester, during which I acted like a clown, sang him every song I knew, followed the complicated directions for his homemade gluten-free mac and cheese, and almost cried when I saw it was only 2:30. I spent the last three hours of the day wondering this: If Hester's mother paid him so much attention and loved him so much, why was he constantly tugging on my sleeve, whining, and giving me not a single moment to read my Nancy Drew book? Why was he so demanding and unable to entertain himself? If I had been his mother, having to conjure up something complimentary to say to the little reprobate four hundred times a day since his birth, I would have worn out faster than a NASCAR tire. How did she do it? Or should I ask, *why* did she do it?

Later that summer, my mother got dressed to go to a ladies meeting, the kind of meeting that required hot curlers and lipstick and the ironing of a pastel-colored dress. She went outside to get in the car and just before closing the front door behind her, turned to give us some last minute instructions. No sooner had she turned back toward the car when she was hit in the face by a blast of cold water coming from our hose. Dear Little Hester stood there in our yard, dousing my southern belle mother from head to toe while she screamed and sputtered. His mother heard the commotion, walked over as calmly as she could, and grabbed Hester's bony hand. As they walked away, mom overheard her saying something.

She couldn't quite make out what it was, but I bet it was something encouraging.

Miss Nelson is Missing

Written by Harry Allard

"Now settle down," said Miss Nelson in a sweet voice. But the class would *not* settle down.

Faced with a mutinous classroom, the normally sweet Miss Nelson grew tired of being mistreated. Her students mistook her kindness for weakness, but, instead of whining about it, she took action. Disguising herself, she gives those kids an experience they will never forget. That experience was Miss Swamp, the strictest teacher they had ever met, a woman who was as mean as she was ugly. She loads them with homework. She cancels story hour. She tells them to keep their mouths shut and to sit perfectly still.
Suddenly, "The kids missed *Miss Nelson!*"

istaking kindness for weakness can happen to even the best children and the children in Miss Nelson's class were no exception. Poor Miss Nelson was only being nice. She was so sweet, after all, reading them stories and making learning fun. It hardly seemed fair her

class abused her so. But abuse they did, and the same thing can happen at home.

Mamas, wanting to be good and kind and perhaps even well-liked by our children, set out to give them as many opportunities as we can, as much of ourselves as we can, the benefit of the doubt as often as possible. But, instead of falling all over us in gratitude, sometimes they respond like Miss Nelson's kids did, by mistaking our kindness for weakness. It's human nature to take things for granted, after all, and children are, if anything, human. Thankfully, *Miss Nelson is Missing* reveals the Great Antidote for when kids take things for granted: I call it The Miss Nelson Two-Step. Allow me to illustrate:

One time Austen and Ben were mutinying like Miss Nelson's class did. They were having a bad string of days, bickering and being ungrateful and they were making life hellacious for the rest of us. Finally, I had to pull the Miss Nelson Two-Step: I told them to move their mattresses into the basement. I allowed them one blanket, one pillow, and the clothes on their backs. I locked their upstairs bedroom door (they weren't in it) so they couldn't access their things. They weren't allowed to play with any of their toys or watch any television until I said they could. The boys were as dumbfounded as Miss Nelson's class was. Who had kidnapped their mother and was the witch who replaced her actually serious?

Yes, she was. It was harder than trying to sew them back into my womb, but I didn't give in. The first day I fed them bread and water for breakfast and told them they could have lunch only if they didn't fight *at all* before noon. They were lambs, and even lambier by dinnertime.

The second day I told them they could earn back one item by lunch if they were good. They were, and earned back their Legos. For every half day they were grateful and kind, they were allowed more privileges. I hated seeing them unhappy, but more than that, I hated seeing them be so mean to each other and so ungrateful for the things we had provided. Miss Nelson quaked inside, but Miss Swamp told her to hold the line.

A week passed before they were allowed back into their rooms, but by then they were sweeter than corn syrup. Stripped of everything but the basics, their sense of entitlement shriveled up like a grape in a heating duct. They emerged from the week with a new appreciation of life and for each other. And for Legos.

No mama likes having to put on Miss Swamp's ugly black wig and pull the Miss Nelson Two-Step. But, as Miss Nelson knew, a short reign of terror freshens the air faster than a Downy drier sheet.

So, the next time your crew starts to mutiny, remember this book. Hard as it is, once in awhile, you may have to channel your inner Miss Swamp. It never hurts to remind them that with Miss Nelson, they had it *good.*

Battle Now or War Later

t seems innocuous enough at first. The first time you call Jonny and he turns around, sticks out his pink boy tongue and runs toward the swimming pool. You don't even get upset. In fact, it's kinda cute. Just look at that chubby little tush wiggling as he boogies away from you.

But what was cute yesterday isn't so much tomorrow, when Jonny's charms have worn off like last summer's tan. At age fifteen, his disobedience is as funny as the evening news and his tush not nearly cute enough to get him off the hook.

Our mistake, of course, was thinking that that teensy battle all those years ago at the pool was just that. Little did we know that that (fuss at the checkout, fit over veggies, bath time squabble) would turn into all out war over curfews, girlfriends, and underage drinking.

So, why do we ignore it? The microscopic etching away of our authority, the resistance to our rules, the ignoring of our 'no's, the mini-standoffs in the back of the van?

We ignore it because we don't realize that children can be

master tacticians and, if given the proper ammunition, they have the ability to prevail from their vantage point at the top of the hill. And, the longer we allow them to, the deeper they embed themselves, fortifying their bunkers and digging trenches and shoveling out a tunnel system that would put the Viet Cong to shame. Given enough leeway, they may flank us on all sides, infiltrate our supply lines and sabotage us before we can say "poisoned porridge."

Our problem is that we are fighting like Revolutionary War era British, lined up in a row in our red (read: here I am, shoot me!) uniforms, muskets poised, bayonets fixed, resigned to our inevitable demise as frontline soldiers while our kids are masters of guerilla warfare, decked out in full jungle camouflage, equipped with M-50s, high-powered scopes, and night vision.

See, we made the mistake of thinking that the tiny skirmish at the pool was an isolated incident. We brushed it off much like the Brits brushed of those pesky colonial farmers and their fuss over tea. Instead of seeing it as an imminent threat to our national security, we overlook it, say it's only a phase, even laugh at it.

And we're surprised when the bombs start falling.

It isn't a war of aggression with every child, of course. Not every kid will come out, battle gear on, weapons at the ready. Depending on their personalities, they may wage a cold war or hold us under siege. The point is to recognize that soldiers come in all forms. And the battles they occasionally wage, no matter how seemingly insignificant, are indicators that something is afoot, that a storm is brewing behind the scenes.

The savvy strategist ought to recognize the value in small

battles because they indicate where the hot zones are. Battles are opportunities. And small ones are easily put down. But even the mildest can escalate into war if we're not on guard.

So, watch your troops, General Mamas. Keep your finger on their esprit de corps. What you think is an isolated incident may be the beginning of your personal WWIII. Pull out your maps, consult your advisors, mingle amongst the tents.

Because, if you don't conquer it when it is small and easily dealt with, you may be looking at years of protracted conflict. Worse, you may raise a dictator that makes Hitler look like a kind, old, chess-playing corner grocer, God forbid. So, be firm. Draw a line in the sand on important issues. And defend your position no matter what.

Someday your country (and your child's future spouse, children, friends, acquaintances, employers, and lawn guy) will thank you.

The Ugly Duckling

Hans Christian Anderson

Unlike his cute, petite, yellow siblings, the Ugly Duckling was gray and large and awkward. No one liked him, not even his own mother. The other ducks snapped at him and the hens pecked at him. They all made his life so miserable that, finally, he ran away. The whole winter, he suffered through not only the cold, but the brunt of the other animal's jokes. But one spring day, he flew toward a flock of beautiful swans and, after looking at his reflection in the water, he realized he was not an ugly and awkward and too big for his feathers duck. He was a brilliantly white and beautiful and glorious swan.

o my great regret we accidentally taped over Anna's birth video. Because of that, and also because she looks so different than the other kids, they often tease her that the lack of cinematic evidence of her birth proves she must be adopted. Her uncanny likeness to my siblings is usually enough to assuage her fears, but occasionally I see a

look in her eye that says, "Mom…?"

Perhaps there is one in every family, a person who doesn't quite fit in, what, in the old days, used to be called a "misfit."

Maybe, like Anna, it's because they don't look like the rest of the family. Maybe it's because they have a starkly different personality from the others. Maybe it's because the other kids have a common trait like a fondness for Marshmallow Fluff or jalapenos that one child doesn't share, that makes her stick out like an ugly gray cygnet in a nest of fluffy yellow ducklings.

I know what it's like to feel like the Ugly Duckling. My best friend growing up was tall and slender, had long blonde hair, smooth tan skin, and wore beautiful dresses her mother made her. I was the shortest person in our class, had fine hair my mother permed into a Hi Fro twice a year, ghostlike skin covered in eczema, and wore dresses my grandmother sewed me out of military grade canvas. I knew I would never garner the attention from boys she did because not only was she perfect, but because I thought wearing striped tube socks with my school-mandated skirt was okay as long as they were both green.

Girls want to look pretty and boys want to look cool because, despite our rhetoric otherwise, appearances are often how we are first judged. This can make our children feel insecure, wondering if their teeth will always be so crooked, their skin always broken out, or their hair always impossible to style.

The UD gives even the most looks-challenged hope, though. He says we're not misfits, we're just on different beauty clocks. Some of us blossom at thirteen and have the other girls jealous of our filled-out bras and boy stares. Some of us don't exit our acne and braces stage until 18. Or 31. Or 42.

At our ten-year high school reunion, I was amazed to see how the gap between the popular girls who blossomed early and the not-so-popular girls who didn't (like moi, pour une petite example) had closed. Most of us seemed to finally have come to grips with our looks, just not in high school when it actually mattered.

Seriously, though, sometimes our beauty clocks are set to go off long after other girls have hatched into cuteness. Some animals are born fuzzy and adorable and others looking like aliens. Eventually we all look like we're supposed to look. If I'd known that I was on the late shift of the beauty clock like the UD was, I might not have fretted as much over my looks and subsequently had the guts to try out for the cheer team or *Fiddler on the Roof* or played my violin with less apology. I might have…

Well, no use going there. It's never too late to understand our own beauty clocks. If we or our awkward and gangly ones feel stuck, unpopular, or downright ugly, we need to remind ourselves that for a long time U-Duck felt the same way. But one day he looked down at his reflection and saw he was gorgeous.

Someday, so will we.

Runaway Bunny

Written by Margaret Wise Brown

"Once there was a little bunny who wanted to run away."

Like Miss Nelson, the Runaway Bunny's mama was one smart lady. When her little bunny threatens to run away, she says that if he does, she will run after him. He says that if she runs after him, he will turn into a fish in a stream and swim away from her. She says that if he does that, she will become a fisherman and fish for him. Over and over, she calls his bluff, until, finally, he tells her that if she continues to come after him, he's going to become a little boy and run into a house. Whereupon the wise mother says, if you do that, I will become your mother and hug you.

"Shucks," says the bunny, "I might just as well stay where I am and be your little bunny."

And he does.

 couple of weeks ago, Cooper refused to help me clean the garage. Granted, it's a terrible job, but it's springtime in Kansas, which means, if you value your vehicle, you will move heaven and earth to create a wind-and-hail-free place for it.

This particular day, all the other children were doing homework and I needed a helper. Cooper, used to working only when the other kids were working, wasn't sure about this whole "help mom by myself" business. He started to cry and complain, but I kept on assigning him small jobs until, finally, I had had enough and told him that he could either work with me without complaining or he could go sit on his bed without his toys.

He chose his bed.

A few moments later, his sister delivered to me this note:

"Der Astin, Ben, Anna, Lani, Emily, Mom, Dad. IM leaving hom. IM runnin away. By."

Because I was too tired from garage cleaning by myself to be nice, I sent a messenger to tell Cooper to have a great time, that we'd miss him, and to be sure to pack his coat because, here on the prairie, it gets cold come winter.

Needless to say, he's still here.

Just like the Runaway Bunny, kids love to try to shock or test their parents. It's a form of manipulation they employ to guilt trip or scare us into giving them what they want. Cooper wanted to go in and play. He didn't want to clean the garage. So, somewhere in his little boy mind, he thought, "I'll teach her a lesson. Watch this!"

Some kids threaten to call 911 or Child Protective Services on their parents when facing disciplinary action. Comedian Russell Peterson says that when a friend suggested he do this, his dad looked him straight in the eye and said, "I might get into a *leetle beet* of trouble, but I also know it's going to take them 23 minutes to get here. In that time, *somebody* gonna get a'hurt real bad."

But, like the Runaway Bunny's mom knew, we cannot allow our kids to have the upper hand in the parent-child relationship. They need to learn early that we love them, but we also know all their tricks. That we are going to raise an eyebrow when they 'go to the bathroom' in the midst of eating their broccoli. That dogs don't even like the taste of homework. That running away doesn't hurt *parents* a bit.

If we let them see our fear (*"What if she really means it this time?"*), we give them the exact location of the chink in our armor, a place you can be sure they will attack often and with great precision.

A child who resorts to such measures needs something. Attention. Reassurance. A boundary. By no means should we ignore their needs. But neither should we positively reinforce their antics by hyper-reacting.

The Runaway Bunny's mother may at first blush seem to be falling for her son's threats, a soft mama who couldn't bear to have him really run away. But the last line of the book tells us she knew what he was up to the whole time. She was just playing along until he circled back to reality.

"Here," she says, "Have a carrot."

1. Do. Not. Negotiate. With. Terrorists.

usie is so sweet. She has this long blonde hair and these lavender eyes that button up when she smiles.

She's so cute it's hard to believe she's a terrorist.

See, she's learned that you hate melodramatic scenes, especially at the store and at your husband's work parties and in hotel rooms late at night because you always have this frantic look in your eyes whenever she creates one.

This communicates to her more clearly than if you had it branded on your forehead that this is, indeed, the Perfect Place For A Fit. Holding you hostage works, you see. She discovered this young, perhaps even while still a baby, when you stuffed that cake into her mouth just to keep her from screaming at that one wedding reception where children weren't invited. Or maybe it was a little later, like that one day you were in Target and she saw these glittery pink ballet slippers that would go so well with her khaki capris and before you knew it, you were forking out $16.99 for shoes you knew perfectly well would last only two weeks and would surely blister her tender heels.

But no price is too much to pay for avoiding what certainly was going to be a dramagasm. She got what she wanted and you got peace, so all's well that end's well, right?

I don't think so.

Call in the SWAT team, we have a terrorist situation.

Have you ever noticed how, in the movies, the hostage holder always loses? In the rare circumstance that a terrorist "gets away with it" for the moment, he's never satisfied. Instead, he tries to pull off a bigger heist. That's when he gets blown off the map.

Not that I'm suggesting *that* as a solution.

Let me put it this way: At first, the stakes with kids don't seem as serious as a terrorist's. No one's going to meet their Maker if you do or do not buy that pink princess purse from the dollar section nor are countries going to topple if you cave and let him have the Bionicle he's screaming for. But know this: Each time we give into "terrorism," our parental kingdom starts to crumble. Once our tiny terrorist learns that we will do anything to keep him happy/quiet, it's the beginning of the end in terms of parental authority.

All that to say, keep your eyes open for local terrorism and, if sighted, squelch it immediately. How you do so is up to you; I'm sure you have some hostage management techniques up your parental sleeve. Whatever you do, though, don't pay the ransom.

Because You. Do. Not. Negotiate. With. Terrorists.

The Gingham Dog and the Calico Cat

By Eugene Field

"The old Dutch clock and the Chinese plate appeared to know as sure as fate there was going to be a terrible spat."

This poem, which North-South Books turned into a delightful hardbound book, is about the mysterious disappearance of the Gingham Dog and the Calico Cat. One day, they had a terrible fight (although no one knows why) and fought until there was nothing left of either one of them. When their owners came home and couldn't find the dog or the cat, they figured burglars had stolen them, but the truth is, "They ate each other up!"

he reader is never told why the dog and the cat were fighting, but the implication in this story is that, whatever it was, it wasn't very important. In fact, all the dog said was 'bow wow' and all the cat said was 'meow' and they were off, "employing every tooth and claw in the

awfullest way you ever saw."

Battles between parents and children or between siblings are often this way. Perhaps you are tired and snap at one of the kids. That child, bruised over your words, responds in kind and, before you know it, the two of you are bickering over... *nothing*. Or, your teenager comes home from school upset over an overdue assignment and you rebuke him impatiently for managing his time poorly and by dinner time you are both cross-armed and fuming.

Considering how much time families spend together, it's amazing we aren't fighting all the time. Statistically, there are 5,040 chances of conflict within our family of eight, for example. Multiply this by the hours in the day, the days in the week, the weeks in the month, the months in the year and we're talking a lot of potential trouble. But most of this, I'm convinced, is over silly things. Give us a bad morning or a few kids with sniffles and before we know it, we are "employing every tooth and claw in the awfullest way you ever saw."

No one wants to fight, of course, nor plans to. We want harmony. We want to choose our battles wisely. But when faced with busy schedules, late bedtimes, and heavy homework loads, there are times families simply get sideways with each other. Exhaustion is often to blame: Tired kids are grumpy kids. Tired parents are grumpy parents. We're baking soda and vinegar. Mix us together and watch us explode.

Discouragement is another culprit. When one of my kids is down for some reason, it's only a matter of time before a fight breaks out. Low spirits or a bad day make us especially vulnerable and unable to handle comments made even in jest.

Sickness is another cause of Gingham Dog and Calico Cat-type behavior. We aren't ourselves. We feel terrible and are uncharacteristically needy. We may expect others to come to our aid or to give us an extra measure of tenderness and we get upset if they don't.

Disappointment, rejection, lack of free time, a too-tight schedule, no schedule at all, or looming deadlines all contribute to potentially explosive situations.

I love the scene in the Emma Thompson version of *Sense and Sensibility* where John Willoughby has just told Maryanne he is leaving for London and has no plans to return to her. Hysterical, she runs out of the room. Her mother is so upset that she, too, runs out of the room crying. When Maryanne spurs Margaret's attempts to console her, Margaret runs away in tears. Stable Elinor, the only one *not* crying, sits on the step with her cup of tea, sighing. The whole scene shimmers with authenticity, because every viewer knows, this is *exactly* how life is.

Our families need ways to avoid ending up like the Gingham Dog and the Calico Cat. Babies need their naps. Children need quiet time in the afternoon. We all need decent bedtimes and a wide swath of margin around our days. We need a good dose of gentleness, forgiveness, and mercy toward each other, especially when things get harried.

The sad thing about the Gingham Dog and the Calico Cat is that, in the end, there was nothing left of either one of them. No one won. Silly arguments are like that. Everyone loses. So, the next time you feel a stress/exhaustion/overload-induced fight coming on, notice what is happening and remember to breathe: You don't want to end up as scraps on the floor.

Millions of Cats

By Wanda Ga'g

"So it happened that every time the very old man looked up, he saw another cat which was so pretty he could not bear to leave it, and before he knew it, he had chosen them all."

The very old man and the very old woman who lived in a nice, clean house were very happy except for one thing: They were terribly lonely. "If we only had a cat," said the very old woman. The very old man sets off to find his wife a cat and, boy, does he. In fact, he finds so many cats, each so lovely and sweet in his or her own way that he can't make a decision. In the end, he chooses them all—"hundreds of cats, thousands of cats, millions and billions and trillions of cats." But his wife is worried. How can they possibly feed all those cats? So the very old couple has to make a decision: Which one will they keep?

As a mama, I can identify with the very old man's dilemma. Mothers are, after all, the Original Decision Makers. Before her child is even born she must decide between natural or medicated child birth, bottle or breast, episiotomy or no. From then on, it only gets more complicated. Going back to work or staying home. Cloth diapers or disposable. Immunizations or not. What babysitter. What kind of schooling. To bus or not to bus. Home made lunch or hot. Organic foods or McDonald's. What age to let them read *Harry Potter*. What kinds of friends. Kinds of allowable clothing. What extracurricular activities to join. When to take the SAT. What colleges to pursue. Car or no car. At what age to let them date. When to let them get their first job. Stances on tattoos and piercings. When to apply for scholarships. Who to let them marry.

Just writing that almost brought on an arrhythmia. Who can possibly make so many decisions in a lifetime?

Mamas, that's who. And usually we do a darned good job. But the very old man in *Millions of Cats* gives us one gentle warning: Whatever we do, *choose wisely.*

Lord knows, he learned that lesson the hard way. Being a kind soul, he couldn't decide between the white cat and the black-and-white cat and the fuzzy gray cat and so on and so forth until, before he knew it, he had picked all trillion of the cats. He soon had a bad feeling about his decision (or lack thereof): One nibble of grass by each kitten cleared off a whole hill. One trillion sips of water emptied a whole pond. How would he and his wife ever take care of all those cats?

Have you ever felt like you've bitten off more than you can chew, like the very old man did? One year we signed up four of the kids for basketball and didn't have a single basketball-free day for a semester. Other times, we've had too many in music lessons or in show choir. Parents are so well meaning, after all. None of us want our children to fall behind or not have the opportunities other children have. A frenetic schedule seems a small price to pay for not missing out on anything, ever.

Or is it? Like the very old man and the very old woman discovered, not being decisive enough always has a price tag. One cat would have alleviated their loneliness. Trillions of cats would have made them crazy.

The very old man and the very old woman were fortunate because their lack of decision-making was resolved with—note this—one simple question: "Which of you is the prettiest?" they ask. All the cats start fighting, each insisting he or she is the prettiest. After the dust settles, only one scraggly cat remains. When asked how he survived, the kitten said, "Oh, I'm just a very homely little cat, so when you asked who was the prettiest, I didn't say anything. So nobody bothered about me." One simple question solved all their problems. They kept that cat and he grew wonderfully fat, happy, and, yes, very, very pretty.

When faced with the decision to add any new "cats" (activities) to my schedule, *Millions of Cats* reminds me to ask myself some important questions first:

Do we *need* this cat?

Is the stress of this cat worth it (sometimes it is)?

If we did not take on this cat, would we feel disappointed or relieved?

Will this cat eat or drink up all our resources?

Does this cat align itself with the things we value?

This is an important question because, if we say we value lots of close family time and the activity in question involves me or my child being out of the house five nights a week, we've got a problem, Houston.

Perhaps the best thing we should ask is the same thing the very old man asked: *Which cat is the prettiest?*

It's a simple question, but one that could save us from "hundreds of cats, thousands of cats, millions and billions and trillions of cats."

Humpty Dumpty

Mother Goose

Humpty Dumpty Sat on a Wall
Humpty Dumpty Had a Great Fall
All the King's Horses and All the King's Men
Couldn't Put Humpty Together Again.

Sometimes, like Humpty Dumpty, moms fall apart.

One time, I had a bad month, a terrible month actually. Every Friday during this month something awful happened: The first Friday I miscarried our baby at sixteen weeks' gestation. The second Friday I cracked my tailbone while picking the kids up from Vacation Bible School. The third Friday, seven-year-old Austen had a severe croup attack and had to be taken by ambulance to the hospital. The fourth Friday I came home to find my dog half-dead in the backyard.

Like I said, it was a bad month. Probably it would make a good country song if you put it to music. I didn't like that month. On the fifth Friday of that month I stayed home with the blinds drawn and banned the kids from eating sharp foods. You get that way when you have a run of Fridays like that.

Then I fell apart.

Maybe it was hormones; mine were certainly askew after the miscarriage, not to mention the sorrow of losing my baby. Maybe it was exhaustion from nearly screaming every time I went to sit… or stand…or lay down. If you've never hurt your tailbone, take it from me: The tailbone is connected to every single part of the body.

I couldn't smile without pain. I couldn't sit or pull myself into the Suburban without tearing up. By the fourth Friday, when I came home to see our puppy, Lizzie, fighting for her life in the back yard, I lost it.

I don't remember much of what happened after that day, only that I felt miserable, slept a lot, and finally had no choice: I had to ask for help; a friend came over, helped me clean my house (those of you who aren't perfectionists have no idea how humbling that is), and told me it was okay to cry.

Which, believe me, I finally did.

eing a mother is a huge responsibility. Huge. It's no wonder we mamas are so hard on ourselves: We're raising people, after all, and it's terrifying. What if we...*mess up?*

Ironically, it's that kind of fear-driven and perfectionistic thinking that leads to Great Falls. We set for ourselves standards so high that even Mother Teresa couldn't reach them, then feel guilty when we get behind on our vigorous seven-days-a-week exercise schedule or resort to buying the party food from Costco instead of making it from scratch.

At the same time, we want to undo the mistakes our parents made, which means never raising our voices or throwing a spatula against a wall or dressing frumpily. Add to that the pressures of a social media-infused world that fills our heads (literally) with pictures of how family life should look (think Pinterest or *Real Simple*) while at the same time fire-hosing us daily with more how-to-mommy articles (many of which contradict each other) than anyone could possibly read in a lifetime. Not to mention the pressure to document every nanosecond of our child's existence in exquisitely crafted scrapbooks.

With WebMD and YahooAnswers and Google, no longer can we blame our mistakes or poor judgements on ignorance. Because the information is out there, *somewhere*, good mamas will stop at nothing in their scouring of the cyberworld to find cures for their child's dermatitis or sour attitude or propensity to misplace his shoes. Or so goes twenty-first century logic.

It's no wonder that we go to bed feeling guilty because, no matter what else we did right today, we served chicken fingers for supper. Again. And it's no wonder, groaning under these sorts of pressures, we sometimes crack.

Rather than wait for a Humpty Dumpty–type fall, though, wouldn't it be better to perform some preventative maintenance on ourselves before things reach a crisis? Just like we take our cars in every 3,000 miles for a tune-up (or maybe it's oil, I forget these things), we need to ask ourselves if our support systems are in place, if we are sleeping enough, if we are eating enough greens, if we are moving our bodies regularly, if we are filling our cups, if we are growing our minds, and if we are feeding our souls.

If not, we shouldn't be surprised if (or should I say, *when*) we fall apart. If we're always running on fumes, burning the candle at both ends, robbing Peter to pay Paul, how can we not? As moms, one of the best, most UNselfish things we can do is to take care of ourselves, to look ahead and prepare in advance for busy, or stressful times. I can honestly say that every time I have fallen apart, big or small, it is because I have neglected my body, my mind, and/or my spirit. Humpty Dumpty fell apart, but we never find out why. We don't come into the story until the critical moment. By the time we even know he's in danger, he's already scrambled himself.

But no one tells us what the extenuating circumstances were. Maybe being an adorable overall-wearing egg didn't pay enough. Maybe he needed something to lean against. Maybe someone was coming to fry him.

Maybe he just needed a nap.

Whatever the case, learn from him. Learn from me. Trust us, falling apart isn't all it's cracked up to be.

The Secret of Mothering

nd now you have reached the chapter in which I divulge to you the Secret of Mothering. Up until now you have most likely thought it was about sacrifice or making a mean lasagna.

Au contraire, chez amies. The key to good mothering is much, much more difficult. Are you ready? Pencil poised? Paper ready?

The essence of mothering is…(drum roll, please):

Naps.

Lots of naps.

Lots and lots and *lots* of naps.

Whenever I go to a baby shower and they play that game where you put your best piece of mothering advice on a tiny scrid of paper, my other mama friends, those who are much more mature than I am, always have these deep offerings:

Cherish the moment. Smell the roses. It will go so quickly. Savor it. Don't listen to your mother-in-law.

Not me, baby. I go for the jugular.

Take naps, I say.

Lots and lots and lots of naps.

Every time that little bundle is sleeping, no matter it's only 8 in the a.m., put your pretty little head down and sleep.

Why do I say this, you ask? How can I be so shallow?

I'll tell you why:

When I had Emily, I popped out of the hospital bed like a piece of toast, went home, and cleaned the house. I already told you about all the visitors we entertained those first two days. By the night my milk came in, I was starting to feel a bit furry around the edges and when the heavenly nectar finally arrived, I was so swollen and miserable (who has time to figure out how to get *that* into *there* with all this *company?*), I could hardly bear myself.

Yes, I looked like an exotic dancer.

No, I did not enjoy it as much as I thought I would.

The first Sunday at church after Emily was born I was talking to a friend and realized I couldn't hear her what she was saying. I could see her lips moving and I had this sick feeling I was answering questions I couldn't hear. It was as if two cups were over my ears and all I heard was the 'wa wa wa' of the teacher in *Charlie Brown*.

I remembered, from my history major days, that sleep deprivation was a common form of torture in certain cultures and now I knew why. I dreamed within dreams, when I slept long enough to have any. I was so tired I fell asleep during sermons, the virgin episodes of ER, and in the middle of conversations.

I prayed, begged, for more sleep. I told God I would give up anything—food, water, bathing—if only He would let me get three hours of uninterrupted sleep.

By the time I gave birth to Anna, the Almighty answered by teaching me something it takes less stubborn mamas only one or two children to learn: When the baby sleeps, I sleep.

I don't care if there's laundry clogging the ceiling fan or an inch of spaghetti on my dishes. I don't care if the carpets are crumby or if the children occasionally have to watch *Looney Tunes* for an entire morning. I don't care if the phone goes unanswered or if we eat sandwiches for dinner. I will sleep and I will feel like a human. I will sleep and I will not feel guilty. I will sleep and I will be a nice person.

That is why I have adapted a quote from my favorite Roman, Julius Caesar:

Veni, Vidi, Nappy: I came. I saw. I napped.

And—at the risk of sounding bossy—you should too.

Chicken Little

FABLE

Chicken Little was clucking along one day when something whacked her on the head. "The sky is falling," she concluded, and went to inform the king. On the way she ran into all sorts of characters who joined her on her journey. But soon they started fighting amongst themselves, so Chicken Little decided to go back home and never got the chance to tell the king that the sky was falling.

ext to conspiracy theorists, moms are the most freaked-out people group in the world. If there is nothing in the news to worry about, we, like Chicken Little, invent something—like swimming pool cleaners or rogue vaccines—to keep us up at night.

My mother gave birth to me under the dark cloud of Haight-Ashbury, and was convinced I would be hooked on LSD and living in a commune with my long-haired flower brothers by the time I hit puberty.

But I did not.

I did not know what Haight-Ashbury was.

Or where.

A generation later, I followed my mother's Chicken Little example, worrying myself sick that, should Emily actually survive birth, she would be missing an arm, have a hole in her heart, or need a plastic bubble. Her childhood sits in my memory like a cavern of dark, unforeseen tunnels of potential disaster, just waiting to be lit by my flashlight of maternal vigilance. I feared dirt because of intestinal worms. I feared bubble baths because of infections. I feared jarred baby food because of botulism. I feared antibacterial soap because of superbugs. I feared music because of back-masking. I feared open windows because of Eric Clapton.

I ran after her like the mother of a child with brittle bone disease until I was too pregnant with Austen to do so without toppling over. But I still kept a sharp eagle eye on her. Panicked at every cough. Bit my nails to a nub.

Five children later, I was flying home from Seattle when, in the course of conversation, I told the elderly gentleman next to me that I would love to take my kids rafting as he was suggesting, except that I was afraid that if one of them fell out of the raft, I wouldn't be able to rescue them, seeing as there are six of them and only one of me.

Ha, he said. They're that unsafe all the time. You just don't realize it.

What? I said. My maternal vigilance isn't what's keeping them alive? How can you be so sure?

That man knew what you and I and Chicken Little don't, that fretting about the sky falling in won't keep it from doing so. The hard-to-digest truth is that we're not in charge of the sky. And all the worrying and panicking and helmet-placing and mouth guard buying won't keep it up where it belongs. The sky doesn't belong to us and, frankly, it isn't our job to manage it. We're only supposed to deal with what actually happens. Not what *could* possibly-in-a-million years happen.

So, let's make a deal, okay? I'll stop looking skyward if you will. Sound good? Pinky swear?

All the sky gazing in the world won't keep it from falling. It's just a good way to get a crick in your neck. And, at some of our ages, we can hardly afford *that*.

The Very Hungry Caterpillar

By Eric Carle

"Then he nibbled a hole in the cocoon, pushed his way out and…he was a beautiful butterfly!"

The Very Hungry Caterpillar started out as a tiny egg on a leaf. One day he wakes up starving, so he eats his way through a whole lot of food. So much food, in fact, that he gets not only a terrible stomachache, but very fat. Then, an amazing thing happens: He wraps up in a cocoon and, two weeks later, emerges, not as a fuzzy caterpillar, but as a completely new creature.

If you think this story is about how mamas need to eat more chocolate cake and lollipops, you may be in for a bit of a disappointment. Because, once we stop drooling over the the dizzying array of treats the caterpillar got to sample, we see that this story is about something far less fattening: Change.

Change is a loaded word. For some mamas, change is as

scary as a dental visit. It represents the unknown, the different, the uncomfortable.

Others embrace change. It's a "get me outta this town/get me a new job/get me a new hair color" good. It entertains the delectable possibilities of fresh starts, new friends, and exciting adventures.

For the Very Hungry Caterpillar, change didn't come easy. First he had to stuff himself with a strawberry, some blueberries, a piece of chocolate cake, a sausage, a slice of salami, a piece of watermelon, a lollipop and a bunch of other things until he felt awful. Then he had to wrap himself in a crusty brown wrapping for two boring TV-less weeks. Then someone recruited him to star in a book full of holes.

Change is hard for humans, too, but what's awesome is that at least it's possible. What if, no matter how hard he tried, the Caterpillar was grounded for life? Most animals aren't given the chance to decide if they want to change or not. They are born with certain instincts and are bound by the laws of nature. But people are different. We can pray for change. We can choose to change. We can get help to change. It's just that, sometimes, it's easier to complain about our Caterpillariness than to do any of those things.

There are times I feel like the Caterpillar. There I am creeping along, my head close to the ground, thinking life will never be any different or get any better. Any forward movement I make, say, to be more patient or more affectionate, is inhibited by my hundreds of legs, my wide girth, my bushy eyebrows. I can see only inches in front of me; I feel trapped and at the mercy of things I have no control over--genetics, my childhood, the family I was put in. Things I blame my stuck-ness on when I feel I simply cannot change. It's easier to sit in my worm hole feeling sorry for or mad at myself than it is to commit to being kinder or to hugging my kids more often.

What if, no matter what our particular struggles are, we were stuck with the habits/hips/chocolate addictions we had at ages 16 or 25 or 37?

Granted, mamas have an extra challenge when it comes to change because, for a season, we seem to be permanent residents of Caterpillarville. We're so busy nursing and trying to get back into non-elastic waist pants that we don't notice that above-the-belly-button t-shirts are no longer stylish or that the previously trendy *chillin'* has been replaced by the much cooler *chillax*. Every day feels like the day before and we are lulled into thinking every day of our lives will be like this day, that we will always have to budget for diapers and carry two extra baby outfits in our purses.

But we won't.

One day we will wake up like the Caterpillar did and sense that things have shifted, that something is afoot. There is a new scent in the air and the sun seems shinier. Perhaps this is the day you send your child off to kindergarten or realize your potty training days are over. Perhaps your clothes feel looser or your hair's natural color has reemerged. Whatever it is, change is in the air. You can't put a finger on it, but you *feel* it. Your head is clearer than it has been in years, you feel a renewed energy, a new hope for the future.

You may not have noticed the cocoon wrapping around you, nor its unwrapping, but, suddenly, there you are, sprouting brilliant indigo and chartreuse wings. Instead of inching along the dirt with nothing but blades of grass in every direction, you are suddenly—and blissfully—airborne, swooping, diving, soaring far over what just yesterday seemed insurmountable obstacles.

So, don't be afraid of change, Mamas. Like The Very Hungry Caterpillar, change can be your friend. Wrap yourself up for a season if you must. Give yourself time to cocoon—cocooning can give you the time you need to reevaluate, to redesign, to grow. But at some point, retract those land-locked legs and stretch those atrophied muscles. Don't believe those who say you are only an overstuffed worm creeping through life on your belly. That you always were impatient. That people in your family aren't huggers. That you are destined to be shaped like your grandmother.

You weren't created for eating dirt; you were made to fly with the eagles. So, go, morph like the caterpillar, eat your way through some pages, if you must. Whatever you do, get out of Caterpillarville.

I won't lie to you. It's not going to be easy. I'm sure if we asked The Very Hungry Caterpillar, she would concur. But, the thing is, we can't: She's too busy soaring over the mountain tops being just who she was created to be to answer such silly questions.

The Country Bunny and the Little Gold Shoes

By Du Bose Heyward

"What did we tell you! Only a country bunny would go and have all those babies. Now take care of them and leave Easter eggs to great big men bunnies like us."

Swift. Kind. Wise.

That's what it takes to be one of the five Easter Bunnies in the Palace of Easter Eggs.

Cottontail is only a little brown country bunny, but she has big dreams. One day, she tells the rich white rabbits and the big, strong Jack Rabbits that when she grows up, she is going to be one of those Easter Bunnies.

They, being the jerks people can be at times, tell her to go home and eat a carrot.

When she grows up and gives birth to not one, but (like bunnies do), twenty-one *baby bunnies all at once, her dreams seem dashed for good. How will she ever become an Easter Bunny with all these children underfoot, with all those toenails to clip?*

So, for a time, Cottontail sets aside her dreams and gets busy at home. She pairs up her children and teaches each pair how to do a job: Two learn to wash dishes. Two learn to sew and mend. Two sing and two paint pictures. Two sweep and two cook. Little by little, day after day, Cottontail trains her bunnies to be independent and responsible.

Which turns out to be a good thing, because one of the five Easter Bunnies is about to retire...

e interrupt this story to say that Cottontail, has got to be, hands down, the wisest mama in all of (children's) literature. For even though the brown Jack rabbits and the rich white rabbits tell her she will never amount to anything, this wascally wabbit is about to prove them wrong.

Back to the story...

Grandfather Bunny, the one who decides who—and who will not—be among the five Easter Bunnies, calls everyone together. The rumor is true: One Easter Bunny has grown too slow to perform his duties. Someone else needs to take his job. But that Somebunny has to fit a demanding list of qualifications: He must be kind. He must be wise. And he must be swift. The brown Jacks with their rippling muscles and the white aristocrats with their sleek fur laugh when Cottontail shows up with her twenty-one children in tow. What a joke, for the prolific Cottontail to think she would ever be considered for this prestigious position.

But the joke is about to be on them. For when Grandfather Bunny finds out how industrious and smart Cottontail has been to raise such a large family so well, he picks not a him, *but a* her *as the new Easter Bunny.*

"Wait!" you ask. "Are you saying that, out of all those qualified rabbits, Grandfather Bunny picked a country bumpkin without a single qualification besides 'mama' on her resume?" Yes, that's exactly what I'm saying. Cottontail, you see, wasn't just swift from chasing children all day, or just wise to have trained her children so well, she was also kind. How else could she have a house where there was nary a cross word or a tear?

The next day, which just happened to be Easter Eve, Cottontail and the other four Easter Bunnies meet at the Palace of Easter Eggs. One basket at a time, they fly out the door, taking goodies to children all over the world.

About the time Cottontail realizes how tired she is and starts looking forward to taking a little basket home to her own children, the old, wise, kind Grandfather calls her to him with a special mission.

"Because you have such a loving heart for children, I am going to give you the best but the hardest trip of all."

A little boy, who lives very far away, has been sick for a whole year and has never complained. Getting his basket to him means crossing two rivers and climbing three mountains.

"But if you get there you will give more happiness than any other Easter Bunny," says the Grandfather Bunny.

Weary Cottontail takes the egg and hops off, crossing first one river, then the next, climbing one peak, then another, and almost reaches the crest of the third when she slips. Down, down all those mountains she tumbles, all the way back to where she started. Landing under a tree, miles from her destination, she realizes her leg is hurt and she can go no further.

Suddenly, there in that far away land, Grandfather Bunny appears.

"You are not only wise, and kind, and swift, but you are also the bravest of all the bunnies," he says. "And I shall make you my very own Gold Shoe Easter Bunny."

He then places a pair of tiny gold shoes on her feet and immediately the pain leaves her leg and strength fills her body. In a couple of leaps, she reaches the boy's house, places the egg in his hand just as the sun starts to lighten the sky. A few moments later, she returns to her well-tended home where her children are sleeping soundly. The garden is neat, the floors swept, the dishes washed, and the clothes clean and nicely hung.

"And the little house of Mother Cottontail can always be told now from the homes of all the other bunnies. Because in a special place on the wall, on a very special hook, hangs a pair of very tiny little gold shoes."

Thus ends the story of frumpy brown Cottontail who, according to the world, was good for nothing but procreation; Sweet Mother Cottontail who had no degree, no skill set, no corporate experience.

Perhaps you, dear mamas, sometimes feel like Cottontail. Like her, you welcome your babies and work hard, teaching and training them, and make a beautiful home for your family. Like her, maybe you find your deepest fulfillment in meeting the needs of the ones you love most. But like her as well, perhaps you have other passions you also want to pursue.

What I love about The Country Bunny, what makes me choke up each and every Easter Eve when I read it to my own baby bunnies, is that Cottontail doesn't have to choose between raising a family and those passions. Having worked hard to train independent and competent children, she is then free with a clear conscience to pursue a dream of her own. In fact, it is *because* of her diligence at home that she is bestowed with the honor of being the fifth Easter Bunny. Without the work she did at home, she never could have proven herself swift, wise, and kind and would never have been qualified for the prestigious job of Easter Bunny.

If you've mourned the death of dreams that were cut short because your babies came too soon or before you had enough money or twenty-one at a time, learn from Cottontail. She proves that having a family and fulfilling dreams are not mutually exclusive.

One day, when you least expect it, you may get an email or a text saying that GFBunny@easter.com is looking for his next go-to girl. She must be swift, wise, and kind. Shifts are long, but wildly fulfilling. Great benefits, including, but not limited to, a free basket of goodies for your own children. Free uniform and gold shoes.

Will you be ready?

The Little House

By Virginia Lee Burton

"Never again would she be curious about the city…
Never again would she want to live there…
The stars twinkled above her…
A new moon was coming up…
It was Spring…
And all was quiet and peaceful in the country."

The Little House had the perfect life. Living in the country, surrounded by cherry trees and green hills, watching her family grow up around her, she couldn't imagine being happier.

But, once in a great while, she looked at the city lights in the distance and wondered what it would be like to live there. One day, much to her surprise, the trucks and roads and, eventually, the lights themselves came to the Little House. Before she knew it, she was stuck smack dab in the middle of a smoky, crowded city. Her family sold her and she fell into disrepair. Before long, no one remembered who she was or what she had been.

Many seasons went by and, just about the time the Little House despaired of ever being happy again, a girl recognized her as her grandmother's house. The girl arranged to have the Little House moved back to the country. When she got there, the Little House got a fresh coat of paint and a new lease on life. It was a spring unlike any she'd every seen before and anything was possible.

ike *The Very Hungry Caterpillar*, *The Little House* is a story about change. Think of these changes as the seasons of motherhood.

A mama's spring is full of hope and promise. It is the greatest "beginning" she will ever know, for who can hold a newborn baby, nuzzle the top of his head, inhale that sweet baby perfume, and not be filled with an overwhelming sense of newness, the knowledge that *this* is what you were born for, that *this* is the beginning of your future, the moment that will hereafter inform everything you do and everything you are?

With the burst of energy this season brings, you are brimming with ideas and ideals, with dreams, looking ahead to every stage of your child's life, mentally planning the great things they will do, the skyscrapers they will design, the symphonies they will compose, the masterpieces they will paint. You wear yourself out staying atop the latest medical breakthroughs and educational opportunities, never relaxing your vigilance for a single moment, so afraid you are of making a mistake. But, so far, you've made none. It's early in the game, you see. You've neither yelled at your toddler nor scarred your preschooler. Life is a flowerbed filled with the fresh, sweet soil of promise, into which you will plant the seeds of your child's future. You anticipate nothing but a rich harvest of healthy and vibrant plants come autumn.

Eventually, the heat of life cranks up, though, and things dry up a bit. It's now the summer of motherhood, the longest season. The thrill of warm weather and crocuses peeking through the snow has worn off and the dewey, unblemished hope of spring is slightly tempered by the knowledge that such perfection can't last forever.

You may be realizing that your children aren't quite what you ordered, that motherhood isn't quite as glamorous as you expected. For, as the baby grows, he starts to do dreadful things like throwing his spoon off his high chair tray or spitting peas in your face. He may run away from you or cry at bedtime. Other babies may have arrived, making the days long and the nights short. Your ideals shrivel under the crushing heat of exhaustion and you find yourself compromising on previously etched-in-stone standards like Positively No Junk Food and (Fill-in-the-blank) Over My Dead Body. Some days it's too miserable out to properly tend your garden, so you let things go a bit, let the teenagers stay up late or eat far too much pizza, let the aphids have their way from time to time.

Just like a farmer, the bulk of a mama's work is done in the summer. The plants you've so tenderly placed in the ground may or may not thrive. Your fingernails are dirty and callouses appear on your knees. You toss out that one fertilizer because it's too harsh and burns your tender seedlings. You toss out another because, despite its initial eco-friendly promise, from the dollhouse size of your cabbage, didn't help at all.

Time passes and a mere six weeks after the moment you decide you simply cannot take another blistering day, the weather cools a touch, just enough to keep you putting one foot in front of another. Sunlight hits at a different angle, painting honey-colored tips on your corn. Your wheat field is a billowing sea of gold. All the planning, seed buying, plot laying, row digging, planting, watering, feeding, weeding, and bug removing is over.

It's harvest time.

No matter how much you wish you'd planted more pumpkins or fewer squash, your garden is what it is. You can't go back. You can only go forward, digging your hands into the sun-baked earth searching for carrots and potatoes and onions, hoping they are well-formed and tasty, yet fearing too much clay and a lack of sand will have stunted their growth. You watch the sky like the farmer you are, scanning weather reports with the diligence of a storm-chaser, praying for a few more dry days, for those billowing black hail-filled clouds to skirt your property to the north, or blow around to the south instead of dumping their loads on all your hard work. Even the morning of harvest, "What if's" fill your mind and nothing is sure.

A mama's autumn is also a time of reflection. Was I too strict or not strict enough? Did I tell my children I loved them enough? Did we have enough family time? Will the lack of piano lessons hurt them for life? Should I have chosen a different form of schooling? Were their friends good or bad influences? Was I a model of what to do or a model of what *not* to do? Even though they seem like decent people at the moment, are they going to rebel the moment they leave home?

Regardless, the calendar says the time for planting is over. From now on, mamas, our job is to see that our fruit is taken to market or made into a pie by a nice country family. It is either good fruit or it is not. It is done and, for the most part, out of our hands, out of the reach of our latest fertilizer or the wisdom from our most recently-read gardening manual. The final days of autumn find mama wishing for the warm and, yes, even scorching days of summer, the long days we spent with our plants, watering, nurturing, coaxing them to life.

It is also a time to prepare for what lies ahead: Winter.

It may come in like a lion or it might come in like a lamb, but come in, it will. As much as we love our children and treasure our days with them, the on-deck parenting eventually has to come to an end. Children leaving home is how the natural order of things goes, just as a bushel of apples must go to market or risk falling into rot at the base of a tree. A mama's winter is when her produce is delivered and she is left with a silent and disturbingly clean home. It is a time to hibernate and to rest our bodies from the many years of tending to other people. Winter may even be a time to grieve—what was, what is, not knowing yet what will be. The future is blank and we don't yet know what life will look like without diapers and essays and college applications and the phone ringing off the hook.

What we need to remember, mamas, is that, like the Little House found, the winters of our lives aren't the end. Just when things seem the darkest and dreariest, just when we feel under the shadows of the skyscrapers of guilt or doubt or sadness, hope arrives. One day we will wake to the rumbling sound of being pulled from our foundations. The next we find ourselves firmly replanted in a most beautiful place. And, despite many years' worth of being out in the elements, we realize our windows and shutters are fixed and we are painted a lovely new shade of pink.

It's called spring, mamas. And it's time to plant.

The Three Little Pigs

FAIRY TALE

e've talked a lot in this book about preparing children for life, about training them to be independent, and about equipping them to live without our hand holding. We've talked about preparing *ourselves* for the winter of motherhood, when the heavy lifting of parenting is over, but before the spring of our post-child life has arrived. Now, the story of *The Three Little Pigs* tells us a little about the actual letting go part.

Mama Pig sends her three piglets into the world with nothing more than a kiss and a picnic lunch. It begs the question, how did she manage to do it with such seeming effortlessness?

1. **Mama Pig prepared herself:** Not only did she *not* fall into hysterics over her children leaving; she was the one who told her boys it was time to move out. This shows us she must have been emotionally ready to let them go. The book *Boys Adrift* by Dr. Leonard Sax (which I ecstatically recommend) is

full of stories of modern mamas who aren't willing to do that. Some moms encourage their sons *not* to leave home. More and more "boys" even in their late twenties are still living at home with mama instead of having families and careers and homes of their own. And that works just perfectly for her: She needs him too desperately to let him go, anyway. Some children are all too happy to have the free rent and the nightly meatloaf supper to leave. The "nest" is simply too cozy. But we mamas shouldn't encourage our children to stay nestled against our bosoms forever. To mix metaphors completely, mamas have to do what Mama Pig did: Gird up their loins and give their piglets a shove out of the nest.

2. **Mama Pig prepared her piglets:** Notice that when the three pigs leave home, the first thing they do is find shelter. One decides to make his house out of straw, so finds a man who sells straw and goes and builds his house. The second pig decides to build his house out of twigs, so goes and finds a man who will sell him some twigs and builds his house. The third decides to build his house out of brick, so finds a man who sells bricks and builds his house. None of them sits around pondering the meaning of life, sweating over what they should do or not do, or trying to "find" themselves. They get busy living. And they do it without whining or running back home to mommy. This tells me that they were prepared at home to hit the ground running once it came time to leave. Perhaps they had classes in House Construction for Dummies or What To Do Once Mommy Isn't Doing Your Laundry, I don't know. Point is, they were prepared.

3. **Mama Pig wasn't afraid of the Big Bad Wolf:** Part

of that preparedness was knowing what to do when the Big Bad Wolf appeared. When he shows up at the three pigs' various houses to eat them, they don't panic. They simply band together and boil a pot of water. When he comes down the chimney to eat them, he ends up being the one on the menu. Somewhere along the line, Mama Pig must have warned her boys that the BBW was a sneaky fellow, someone to avoid at all costs. When he showed up, as she predicted he would, the boys knew exactly what to do. Mama Pig's sons weren't afraid because they were prepared and I suspect they were prepared for other BBWs in life, too: Debt, dark alleys, manipulative girlfriends, frat parties, black ice, unscrupulous salespeople, power surges, brown recluses, and pyramid schemes, to name a few.

Mama Pig made it look easy, but we know saying goodbye never is. When our teenagers start flapping the wings of independence, rather than shushing them up, stuffing them with more worms, and lining the nest with more fluff, we'd be better off to follow in Mama Pig's cloven hoof prints, preparing them (and ourselves) the best we can and shooing them out the door.

When the Big Bad Wolves of fear and doubt come knocking, we'll just tell them they can huff and puff all they want, but we're not falling for it. Not by the hair of our chinny chin chins.

The Old Woman Who Lived in the Shoe

MOTHER GOOSE

There was an old woman who lived in a shoe.
She had so many children, she didn't know what to do;
She gave them some broth without any bread;
Then whipped them all soundly and put them to bed.

hort of the whipping part, it's tempting, isn't it some days, to do what the Old Woman in the Shoe did? To slap some peanut butter on toast and plop those fussy babies in their cribs, corral the wild toddlers and send them to their rooms, and shoo those restless teenagers down to the basement, days we have so many children/chores/pressures "we don't know what to do?"

When Emily, Austen, and Ben were little, I was more tired than a convict after a complicated escape and each day was an Olympic event called "Survive until 5:30."

I spent every ounce of kinetic energy doing that until the glorious hour in which Ian got home and could rescue me for a few blessed minutes. I fantasized about eating food that was still hot, dreamed of sleeping without interruption, and relished the few showers I got without an audience of three toddlers who I am pretty sure were laughing at my post-pregnancy overhang.

We all have days we want to crank open a can of soup and feed the kids and tell them it's 7:48 even though it's only 5:21. So, what are we to do when these days come, as they undoubtedly will?

For starters, we can pray.

Oh God, help this be only the bean burrito she ate for dinner and not the start of a Rotovirus that will run through the entire family until we only have one unviolated pillowcase and a single clean washrag left in the house.

Lord, please don't tell me we are sixty miles away from civilization and I have forgotten to pack the baby's diapers.

Heavenly Father, I will do anything if only you will make this baby stop crying.

Lord, have mercy on me, I beg you to make something yummy appear in my pantry before 5 p.m.

God, please, just five more minutes of sleep.

Sometimes God answers prayers like these in our favor and sometimes He doesn't. But one thing is sure: However tiring or scary the situation we're in, it won't last. Everything we encounter, from flu bugs to sewer line breaks to a houseful of children with chicken pox will—like the cliché says—pass. Which is why someone really smart wrote it.

One day, long before we are ready for it, our children will

be out of the house and on their own and our "shoes" will be empty. The clock will tick and ten minutes later, it will tock. Our homes will not only be clean, but will *stay* clean. Leftover lasagna won't be gobbled up by ravenous teenaged boys. Our makeup won't be pilfered by prepubescent girls. We will open a cabinet and find a pile of Hostess cherry pies that we can eat at our leisure, without sneaking them into a shirt cuff and running to our rooms. Our cars will no longer smell like McDonald's French fries and little boy feet.

So enjoy it while you can, fellow Old Women in Shoes. Enjoy all those children. And their chaos. And their mess. And their noise. And their interruptions. And their never-ending questions. And their wet towels on the bathroom floor. And the couch cushions pulled off the couch for the hundredth time. And the six gallons of milk in the already-crowded refrigerator. And the apples that you paid good money for, but that lie shriveled in the bottom of the fruit bowl and the pizza boxes that fill your recycling bin and the chattering of little girls behind the wall when you are trying to sleep and the linen closet filled with toys that has no room for your sheets and the forty coats that are threatening to pull your coat hooks from the wall.

Soon all that will end. And, if you're anything like me, you'll miss it like heck when it does.

Miss Rumphius

Written and Illustrated by Barbara Cooney

"That is all very well, little Alice," said her grandfather, "but there is a third thing you must do."
"What is that?" asked Alice.
"You must do something to make the world more beautiful."

If you don't have your own dog-eared and spit up-covered copy of this book, drop everything, unlatch the baby from your breast, and run to your nearest book store. You simply must *own it.*

This book is like having tea with your best friend at the quaintest tea shop in town, sitting at a table topped with jewel-colored Gerbera daisies and sinking your teeth into a vanilla cream puff dusted with powdered sugar. It is the equivalent in inspiration of Puccini wafting from the balcony of your Italian villa.

Miss Rumphius wasn't always Miss Rumphius, you see. She used to be a little girl named Alice who lived by the sea with her grandfather who sometimes let her paint the skies in his landscape paintings. She loved her grandfather very much and wanted to do just what he had done with his life: She wanted to see the world and live by the sea. When she told him this, he told her that her aspirations were all well and good, but that there was yet another thing she must do: She must find a way to make the world a more beautiful place.

The question was…how?

n the thick of diapering and scrap booking and reading bedtime stories, it's easy to forget that mothering isn't about any of these things.

Nor is it about Kodak moments, tiny blonde curls, or the appearance of new pearly teeth.

Mothering is about doing what Miss Rumphius' grandfather told her to do: Making the world a more beautiful place.

The thousands of everyday tasks associated with raising children, important as they are, are not ends to themselves. Neither are the sentimental milestones and the memorable moments that choke us up.

Mothering involves these things, for sure, but it is not *just* about these things.

I overemphasize this point because it's easy for mamas, especially in the early years when knee deep in babies and exhaustion, when the initial bloom of mothering has worn off, to grow discouraged. It's easy, at times like these, to think that being a mama is about as fulfilling as running the Ferris Wheel at an amusement park, one thing, over and over, la-dee-da, here we go again…

But a mama with a Miss Rumphius mindset knows better. Here's why: Inspired by her grandfather's challenge to make the world a more beautiful place, Miss Rumphius moves to the sea, plants a few flower seeds around her house, but ends up bed bound for months after injuring her back. How will she ever find out how to make the world a better place now?

One spring day, when she is finally feeling better, she goes on a walk and what do you think she sees? Lupines everywhere. "I don't believe my eyes!" she cries. "It was the wind that brought the seeds from my garden here! And the birds must have helped!"

Suddenly, Miss Rumphius knew exactly how to make the world a better place. She buys two bushels of lupine seeds and walks around her village, flinging seeds wherever she goes. From then on, every spring, pink, purple, and blue lupines pop up everywhere—by the church, next to the school, along stone walls. Before long, Miss Rumphius became known as The Lupine Lady. At long last, she found out exactly how she was to make the world a more beautiful place.

Marti Barletta, in her book, *Marketing to Women*, says that the number one thing a woman wants in life is to make the world a better place. The second thing she wants is to see her children succeed. A mama with a Miss Rumphius mindset can do both at the same time by looking beyond the often-tiresome and sometimes-irksome tasks associated with motherhood and seeing her job as one of the best possible ways to make the world a better place.

For, as mothers since antiquity could attest, behind every history-changing man and woman was a mother doing ordinary, every day work. Sandwich making. Dinner planning. Sock sorting. Wiping runny noses and catching vomit in plastic buckets is just part and parcel of raising the next Teddy Roosevelt or Johann Sebastian. In the midst of the 52nd attempt to clean up the glitter from our daughter's art project or our grief over someone carving "coop is #1" in the dining room table, it's easy to forget that.

What gets us through the tedious parts of motherhood is this mindset, for it turns the mundane into the spiritual. So, you did a load of wash, set crayons on the table, read the kids a book, and roasted a chicken for dinner…again. Who cares? What does it really matter? In a hundred years, will anyone remember what you did or if you included a green vegetable with tonight's meal?

Well, yes, actually.

Except for the vegetable part.

Something magical happens to the ordinariness of motherhood when we start to think like Miss Rumphius. Our work starts to transcend the laws of mathematics. Two plus two begins to equal 6, and love, rather than being diluted with the arrival of each child, in some inexplicable way exponentially expands.

The Cheerios strewn on the carpet and the yellow stains around the necks of the baby's undershirts are not just messes, but part of a holy work. As we set the table, load the dishwasher, wipe up yet another glass of spilled apple juice, the building blocks of a child's life are laid down; one at a time, some placed oh-so-carefully, some haphazardly, and a child is built.

If we see mothering as a chore to be merely endured, that is exactly what it will become. But, if we see it as a way to make the world a better and more beautiful place, if we realize the significance of raising spiritual beings, it will be a venture with eternal consequences. No task will ever be without meaning, no chore mindless. Like a marathon runner who suddenly glimpses the finish line in the distance, a mom who knows where she is going will not falter as often as her running mate who is thinking of nothing but her stabbing side stitch and blistered toes.

Of all the things we do to make the world a better place, what can surpass raising the next generation? Although no one but a fool would say it will be easy, what could possibly be more important than loving, training, encouraging, cleaning up after, bathing, feeding, and praying for the future leaders, musicians, artists, historians, engineers, craftsmen, and writers of tomorrow?

I can't think of anything.

Can you?

Your 75th Birthday Party

he day dawns sunny, the crystal, cornflower blue of your grammy's eyes. Your favorite people are present: The man who has loved you since puberty. Your precious children and their lovely spouses. Gorgeous grandchildren. Fat little great grand babies. Your best friend from kindergarten, if you're lucky. A three-tiered lemon cake topped with vanilla butter cream frosting and fresh raspberries rests under a tent in your garden. A nearby table with a flowing tablecloth is groaning with the presents piled on top of it. And they're all for you.

It is August of your 75th year and this is your birthday party.

For years you have passed the occasion with barely a nod. Birthdays have meant less and less each year, reminders—not of life getting more and more fantabulous like it used to be—but of you getting older and weaker and achier. So, most of the time, you have simply chosen to barely acknowledge them.

But today is different. Your children have flown in from Georgia, Washington, and Toronto to honor you. Vases of cream-colored roses and baby's breath top each table. Your sons are grilling tandoori chicken (your favorite meal) and spicy shrimp (your second favorite meal) while your daughters serve fresh Greek salads and ruby red strawberries with their stems intact. Strains from your grandchildren's sweet laughter fill the air. Bach floats out of a speaker hidden under a table somewhere. White twinkle lights wind their way through the tulle canopies that cover the yard and offer a gentle, but festive glow to the party.

Suddenly a spoon taps on a champagne glass. Someone clears his throat. It is speech time and already four or five people are standing in line to speak.

You, bare-shouldered in a white shimmery dress, wait. Secretly you love parties. Especially ones where you are the center of attention. But you don't dare let anyone know. So you wait, impatiently—but a bit nervously—to hear what those nearest and dearest to you have to say.

How will your oldest daughter sum her relationship with you? Did your relationship fracture over her decision to marry early? Or did it cause you to be closer than ever?

What will your youngest son say about your mothering? Were you always preoccupied when he tried to tell you about his rambling dreams? Or did you drop what you were doing, clamp eyes on him, and *listen?*

What stories will your best friend tell? Will she tell the one about where you spent the better part of a girls' weekend lost on the 405 freeway in Seattle? Or about how you used to gather boy germs on the playground and played with dolls who were named Barfy and DiDi, based on their opposing bodily functions? Or will she say that you never let her get a word in edgewise and one-upped her every story?

What will your husband say about your good/bad/ugly years together?

Will your brother recall you as being uptight and bossy, or as making the worst of situations fun?

Will your sisters speak of your empathy or of your judgmental spirit?

Will nieces and nephews tell stories of your funny emails to them while they were in college, or sit silent in their chairs stewing over your lack of interest in their lives?

Most of us reading this chapter aren't anywhere near our 45th birthday parties, much less our 75ths. But now is the time to lay the groundwork for a good one. To plan it, even. Stephen Covey says we should begin with the end in mind and backwards plan from there. Imagining the 75-year-old you may change the course of the 35-year-old you. Life may become more purposeful. Relationships might be held more tenderly.

Consider, mamas, the woman, wife, mother, daughter, sister, and friend you are today. Ask yourself, when it comes time to pull up the covers of life, will you be proud of being the kind of person you are today? Did you live a life of service, kindness, and empathy? Were you gracious? Were you liberal with hugs and stingy with criticism? Did you love intensely, ask for help when you needed it, pray for guidance?

If your answer to any of these questions is even a remote yes, grab a glass: You've got some celebrating to practice.

Madeline

by Ludwig Bemelman

> "But the biggest surprise by far—*on her stomach was a scar!*"

Although Madeline is the smallest girl of the twelve who live in the old vine-covered house in Paris, she makes up for her size with courage. When she has to have her appendix removed, she proudly shows off not only the toys and candy and dollhouse from her father, but her newly acquired scar. It's no wonder that after visiting her in the hospital, the other girls scare Miss Clavel half to death by crying out, "Boohoo, we want to have our appendix out, too!"

hen I was twenty-nine, I had a Madeline-type experience.

It all started with this fantastic sundae. First I put a freshly baked brownie in a bowl. Then I covered it with a scoop of vanilla ice cream and topped it with a mountain of hot fudge. All the vanilla melted down into the brownie and the hot fudge soaked down into the ice cream and I ate it very, very quickly.

The next morning I woke in terrible pain. It felt like the brownie was trying to kill me from the inside out. We rushed to the hospital where, like Madeline, we found it was my appendix, which apparently hadn't enjoyed the sundae as much as I had. Now I understood why Madeline cried in her bed that night in Paris. Appendixes gone bad *hurt*.

Thanks to modern medicine, I have only three tiny scars as opposed to the wide gash that got Madeline so much attention, but that's okay. Scars show I'm not perfect, you see, and I'm usually more interested on keeping the illusion intact than showing them off like Madeline did.

Physical scars are one thing, but emotional scars aren't easy to expose, either. We might hide them behind a humorous exterior or under layers of accomplishments, busyness, or charm, but not many (unjailed) people I know go around flaunting them Madeline style.

It's too bad because many interesting, deep people are those who have scars. They know what suffering is. They know life can be messy. They have spent time analyzing how things got to where they are, trying to figure out ways to mend situations, and are learning how to overcome obstacles. With this comes an emotional grit that is not developed in a person whose worst experience in life is having to wait twenty minutes in line for her Xanax.

Good stories, the kind editors buy and publish, are about scarred people, not those who have arrived at the end of their lives unscathed. Story is about movement and, in the good ones, the main character isn't static. She's not the same person at the end that she was at the beginning. If she is, you don't have a story. Not one anyone will read anyway. Good stories have crises. They have stakes. And those stakes are raised, then they are raised again. Characters are put in situations they can't get out of. That's what keeps the reader turning pages until three in the am. The climax of the book, the point where the tension can rise no further, happens about 3/4 of the way through the story. That's almost the end of the book, folks. Note that.

Then, and only then, is there resolve, the "denouement" for you fancy writer types. Then and only then do the pieces of the puzzle start to slide into place. Then and only then do the various story threads start to tie off. Only then does the reader feel satisfied.

Our stories—for our lives *are* stories, aren't they?—are punctuated with scars, ugly knobby ones we may have hidden our whole lives. Much as we might like to, in the computer of life, we can't shred our Word file and start over with a fresh document. There's no White-Out. No backspace button. No cut and paste. No delete. But, rather than letting this depress us, we might want to consider how we can best use our divorces, deaths, illnesses, miscarriages, broken hearts, lost jobs, failed businesses, embarrassing bankruptcies, rebellious children, humiliating experiences, shattered dreams, chronic pain, and broken families. Will we script a dramatic, depressing ending or a beautifully redemptive one?

Rather than denying our scars, maybe we'd be better off doing what Madeline did, raising our shirts (not *too* high, now) and proudly showing them off. For our wounds-turned-scars can teach us much about ourselves—why we are like we are and why we react like we do. Or, as in my case, why I don't like chocolate anymore. They can give us empathy for others who have suffered. Like snowflakes, no two scars and no two stories are alike. How will we know who needs our story if we keep rubbing it with Vitamin E or hiding it behind thick scarves?

So, maybe instead of allowing them to disfigure us for life, we should embrace our scars, like Madeline did, recognizing that they are momentous (perhaps even pivotal) chapters in the stories of our lives.

Stories, I remind you, that aren't done being written just yet.

Epilogue: Your Story

"Stories never really end...even if the books like to pretend they do. Stories always go on. They don't end on the last page, any more than they begin on the first page."

CORNELIA FUNKE, AUTHOR OF **INKSPELL**

As I sit on the couch writing, Elenia and Cooper are upstairs taking showers, fighting over who gets the dry towel. Leftovers from dinner are congealing in individual bowls on the counter because someone forgot to run the dishwasher earlier. The older boys are upset with me because I dared ask why they were playing *Halo* instead of doing their homework.

When a dear friend of mine heard I was writing a mothering book he said, "Amy, just tell what you know to be the *absolute truth* about mothering."

It sounded easy at the time, but, on a night like tonight, the truth about mothering eludes me like fit thighs.

What is the absolute truth about mothering?

I have absolutely no idea.

Eighteen years into it, I still freak out when my kids throw up.

What I do know (not much), and what I have learned (in all the hardest ways possible), is that mothering is not an endeavor easily distilled down into pat answers, tidy boxes, and simple formulas.

During the few moments a year I can momentarily quiet my fears and worries, I realize it is the wildness and woolliness of motherhood that comes closest to answering my friend's challenge. The truth about mothering is that there's no one way to do it. In fact, what makes it an adventure, what makes it such a rewarding undertaking is *not* knowing exactly how it's done, the jumping out into the unknown without a chute, the plunge into waters I'm not sure will be bath-warm or shark-infested.

No mama I know ventures there without trepidation, nor does any one kind of mama have it figured out: Not Pooh Mamas. Not Rabbit Mamas. Not even (sigh) Owl Mamas.

What do we do, then? We imperfect, yet stunningly unique and beautiful mamas?

According to the Velveteen Rabbit, Being Real is a good place to start. The Saggy Baggy Elephant chimes in to remind us that part of Being Real is accepting our bodies, sags, bags, and all. Inspired by Madeline, we nervously start sharing our scars and, thus, begin rewriting the stories of our lives with a little more compassion.

Like the Little Engine, we wonder if we can do it. We look at the mountain ahead and cringe. *I thought I could* seems awfully far away. We have days like Alexander did where nothing goes right and days like Max did where we have to stare right into the yellow eyes of our worst fears and see who's boss.

We have times we feel as alone as Horton perched in his tree, icicles growing from his toes, wondering just what we signed up for. We have others where we go to grab Harold's purple crayon in our back pocket only to find it isn't there. It is, in fact, melted to the inside of the dryer, covering our new white tank top with a waxy lavender tie-dye. We have times, like the Little House, where the changes in our lives threaten to undo us or where we want to run away like Lazy Mayzie and leave our worries behind. We have to summon the energy to discipline our houseful of Curious Georges and fight hard against the discontent that nearly ruined that nasty fisherman's wife. That much is given.

But, be assured, dear mamas that as certain as these kinds of days are, so too are other kinds of days. Days that we feel stretched out like The Mitten, but suddenly find ourselves floating through a crystal blue winter sky, untethered by prickles or worries. Days we revel in the love and support of our Ya-Yas. Days we realize we have morphed from fat squishy caterpillars into gorgeous butterflies. Days we find out we've been voted the next Easter Bunny and days we "pwn" our naughty crew like Miss Nelson did hers. Days we woo back our Runaway Bunnies and days our Owl Babies hoot and holler in sheer happiness when we get home.

So, go, make this world a better place, mamas. Like Miss

Rumphius, scatter your seeds far. Trust.

Because this story is yours and I pray it ends like all the good ones do,

"...and they all lived happily ever after."

The ~~End~~ Beginning

Acknowledgements

When a book is published, it is through the work and sacrifice of no small number of people and this one is no exception.

A huge shout out to all you mamas who patiently answered my time-sucking survey and your children who probably went hungry while you did so. I am in your (and their) debt for your honesty and vulnerability as you helped me put some flesh on the 'real truth' about being a mama.

Thank you to my Facebook friends who were regularly pummeled with random mothering questions, especially those who helped me brainstorm the title for this sack of words.

Thank you to Dorothy Moran, my champion. Her faith in my writing is what started this journey.

Thank you to Kim Strotz, a Whole Mama if ever there was one. Dear friend, wonderful mama to five incredible children, and the most encouraging person I've ever known. She left this world decades too soon. How I miss you, girlfriend.

Thank you to my awesome coach, Dr. P., who gave me the challenge to write what I know to be the absolute truth about mothering and who held my arms up when the going got rough.

Thank you to my unofficial encouragement team: My Trinity Covenant Church family, my Whole Mama subscribers, my brave coaching clients, and my behind-the-scene buttresses, without whom this would have remained nothing but an impossible-to-decipher Scrivener file.

Thank you to my precious and irreplaceable Ya-Yas, who know who they are. Without you, I'd be broke from the therapy bills.

Thank you to my own mama, who instilled in me a love of old, dusty bookstores and the stories inside them, and to my dad for teaching me to love words and what a full floating rear axle is.

Thank you to my babies Emily, Austen, Benjamin, Anna, Elenia, and Cooper, for allowing me to tell our stories to complete strangers, for being guinea pigs to my parenting theories, for loving me as I stumble down the road to grace, and for making your own quesadillas and watching lots of Netflix streaming while I finished this book. You make getting out of bed worth it.

Finally, thank you to Ian, my truest companion on this wild and woolly journey, for saying I could, and whom, I'm sure, would concur with Louisa May Alcott who said: "She is too fond of books, and it has turned her brain."

Soli Deo Gloria

www.ingramcontent.com/pod-product-compliance
Lightning Source LLC
Chambersburg PA
CBHW051752040426
42446CB00007B/327